# THIS SIDE OF THE VEIL

# THIS SIDE OF THE VEIL

KARINA CHEAH

NEW DEGREE PRESS
COPYRIGHT © 2020 KARINA CHEAH
*All rights reserved.*

THIS SIDE OF THE VEIL

ISBN 978-1-64137-949-6 *Paperback*
    978-1-64137-761-4 *Kindle Ebook*
    978-1-64137-762-1 *Ebook*

*for Kelsey*

*and the sunshine that you brought*

*and still bring*

*to every day.*

# CONTENTS

| | |
|---|---|
| Author's Note | 9 |
| 1. The Things We Keep | 15 |
| 2. What Are Words | 29 |
| 3. To Follow a Star | 51 |
| 4. Pineapples | 71 |
| 5. don't burn out. | 85 |
| 6. resolution... | 105 |
| 7. Dear Kelsey, | 121 |
| Acknowledgments | 131 |
| Appendix | 133 |

# AUTHOR'S NOTE

On the evening of May 7, 2019, I stood in the Fager Lounge at Colgate University, smoothing my hand over the last four pages of my portfolio for my creative nonfiction writing workshop. I was there partly out of obligation, because the class reading was required by my professor, but I also truly wanted to read some of the work I'd spent the past two months honing and trimming.

I'd chosen a piece I'd written as a tribute to a friend—my friend Kelsey who unexpectedly passed away in a horseback-riding accident at the end of July 2018—out of a hope that if I read about her to a room crowded with familiar faces, I would feel resolved. My healing journey would be complete within the seemingly remarkable span of eight months.

Spoiler alert: It wasn't.

I felt better, to be sure. I was, and still am, glad I chose to read from that essay, even though it was difficult to stand in front of a crowd and lay myself bare to them about a loss that had affected me so deeply. An element of healing came from sharing my experience and what I loved about Kelsey with the world. But the ribbon tied around the whole eight months of wrestling with those feelings of pain and loss and even guilt—it didn't come. I felt better but not complete.

***

Everyone knows about the Kübler-Ross model for grief. If they don't know it by name, they might have heard of it in terms of the five stages of grief: denial, anger, bargaining, depression, and acceptance. There is a perception that there is supposed to be a movement through the stages—not necessarily in that order or even in a linear sort of fashion, but that a person will move through the stages and eventually come out feeling resolved and okay on the other side. That once you come to acceptance, you've accomplished something. You will have checked the box of grief and moved on from the loss.

To a certain extent, I think this is true. I'm not about to try and debunk a well-established psychological framework with one short story collection; I don't think that's a productive use of my or your time and especially not through the medium of fiction. What I will say, however, is that I don't think there is a required order of stages through which a person needs to pass to begin to understand a loss that they've experienced.

It's nice to be able to put a term to an emotion I'm feeling, but I have trouble with the idea of being presented with a framework for grieving. I worry that if I miss a step, I feel as though I'm doing something wrong—as though somehow, I'm grieving incorrectly. And grief is such a deep, personal process that I can't imagine anyone wanting to feel that they are doing it wrong.

Yet grief is also so universal, and such a widely understood emotion, that it's also a comfort to know other people are going through it, even if they are experiencing it differently than you. Loss has a ripple effect; for every person who's lost, at least one person will feel it, and at least one person will feel for the person who's feeling it. And that doesn't begin to account for those who haven't lost someone today but have or know someone who has lost someone in their lifetime.

So grief is a universal thing, but at the same time, it is so deeply personal that I can't even begin to understand what it would be like for my friends who have known and lost people they loved. Everyone experiences and processes it differently. I guarantee that the grieving processes experienced by Kelsey's family and friends were all different from mine, even if only slightly—and even as we were all missing the same person.

\*\*\*

In August 2018, I threw myself into life again—finished my trip with my family (I was abroad when I found out about Kelsey), came home, packed for school, and dived headfirst into my sophomore year at Colgate. But there wasn't a single day that went by, or that goes by now, when I didn't think about Kelsey. I kept the program from her service pinned up over my bed at school and the gold horseshoe she spraypainted for me on my desk in my dorm. Life at Colgate was and still is always so busy between classes and riding and homework that at the beginning of that semester, I rarely had time to dwell on what had happened over the summer. I assumed that I was doing fine.

When course registration for the spring came around, I needed another workshop for my creative writing minor, so I applied to and registered for the nonfiction one on a whim—although it was in part because I wanted to challenge myself, as I'm used to working with fiction. We were tasked with three essays throughout the semester—two short and one long. When it came time to write the long one, it was as though I had always known what I was going to write.

I wanted this piece to be my way of processing, my way of moving past what had happened; a symbol of healing, if you will. Call it corny, but I'm a writer. Everything is a symbol if you think about it for long enough. And in a way, it was, but it also wasn't. That essay still marks a point in my grieving journey, but it's not the culmination of my healing. If anything, it was just the beginning.

The longer I wrote, the more doors I opened as to what was really happening in my head. Because assuming that I was fine was my first mistake. That essay is probably one of the most difficult pieces I've ever written—in part because it is so personal but also because of the complexity of grieving that I had unwittingly pushed to the side.

There were things I didn't realize I was thinking until they landed on the page. Many of them were and remain unresolved. Grief, guilt, anger, so many other unnamed emotions blend and swirl together in those pages. But there was something soothing about reminiscing and writing, even if those memories hurt a little now that Kelsey is gone. The happy memories are still there, but there's always that little sting reminding me we'll never have the chance to make more.

That's how it feels to me, anyway. For some people, reminiscences may be too painful to look back on. For others, reminiscences are the key to their healing journey. And that's okay.

✳✳✳

This collection marks another point in my journey of grieving and healing. It is not a resolution. It's been a space where

I can explore the avenues behind the doors opened by my essay, happily ensconced in the realm of fiction where I am less inhibited by the facts of what happened to me. I don't know where or if it fits into one of the Kübler-Ross stages of grieving, and I don't think it needs to. What matters is that it's helping me understand the things I've been internalizing, those emotions I haven't spoken about or dealt with. Writing has always been a way for me to understand myself, whether I'm deeply confused about something or using it to help me process something as big as a loss like this.

This collection holds the stories of several characters, none of whom are related to each other—from a seven-year-old girl to a grieving college-age man. It is by no means representative of every experience one might have in response to a loss. There are faiths and practices I haven't delved into and experiences that I will never understand. But I am not here to capture every single story about loss and grieving. I am here to try and make a positive impact—even if that is only for one person.

What I hope for you, reading it, is that you can see yourself in some or all of my characters. I hope you can see that there are countless ways to grieve and that if you're working through the aftermath of a loss, you can know that your process of grappling with it while trying to push forward with your life fits right in with everyone else's. I hope that you can connect with my characters and know that even if your experience is personal, there is a universal understanding as to what grief means. I hope that my characters might even be able to help you in some way.

There isn't always a neat resolution, even if you want one. And yet, improbably, life goes on.

Nora McInerny closed a TED talk about how people deal with grief with this quote: "Yes, absolutely, they're going to move forward. But that doesn't mean they've moved on."[1] And I love this approach. There is something so permanent about moving on, something in it about moving past someone and leaving them behind. But the reality is, we take everything with us, two months or two decades later. We move forward.

Some people will write and others will talk. Some will contemplate and process alone before going to others with their thoughts. Some will talk to friends or parents or therapists right away. Some will alter their daily routines to make space for their person now that they are gone. Some will do one thing, every year, on a birthday or the anniversary. All of these ways of holding on—the little things we do for our people—they are equally valid ways of grieving as we pick ourselves up and put our lives back together, figure out how to live when a piece of the puzzle is missing. There is no right or wrong way to grieve, as long as you're going about it in a way that is safe and comfortable for you.

Some of these things will carry through the rest of our lives. Some of them will peter out. But we never stop missing our person or people. We move forward, yes. But we don't always move on.

And that's okay.

---

1  *TED*, "Nora McInerny: We don't 'move on' from grief. We move forward with it." November 2018, video, 14:43

1.

# THE THINGS WE KEEP

*Charlotte, 7, just outside Toronto, 2003*
*"I don't understand. Don't the good ones always get to come back?"*

Mama is supposed to call me in for dinner. Right at six, every day for the past two years. Ever since I turned five and was old enough to go play in the yard by myself, that's been the routine. Mama really likes her routines.

I'm outside, sitting on the grass in the yard, drawing a picture in the dirt. Usually I run around and make up a game for myself when I'm outside, but I finished my game for today. I don't know what time it is, but it feels later than six, because the traffic is quieter and it's darker and a little cooler outside. The birds have gone quiet and the mosquitoes are coming out, and I think I'm hungrier than usual.

I get up, brush the dirt off my pants, and drop my stick in the grass. My picture is only half finished, but I'm hungry and I want to know what happened to Mama. Mama doesn't usually forget about her routine.

The deck door is open but the screen door is closed, the way Mama always leaves it, so I go into the kitchen and look around. Plates are stacked on the table and the silverware is in a pile. I can smell tomato sauce and pasta, but I can't find Mama. The phone is missing from the counter, though, where it usually sits in its holder.

I wander into the living room, where Papa is sitting on the couch reading, but he looks up and smiles when he sees me. "Hi, sweetie."

"Hi, Papa." I sit down on the couch next to him, swinging my legs back and forth. "Do you know where Mama is? I'm hungry."

"Well, Auntie Lillian called, so I thought we should wait till she comes back so we could all eat together like we usually do." Papa smiles and ruffles my hair, and I duck out of the way and swat at his arm.

"Papa, don't do that." I fold my arms and frown at him. "Is Mama going to be done soon? I'm hungry."

"Sorry, sweetie." Papa smiles. "Let me go see where Mama is."

I wait on the couch, still swinging my legs back and forth. I want to eat, but I don't want to start without Mama and Papa, because they tell me we should always eat dinner together, so we can be a real family for that time. They work a lot, so they like it when we can all be together for dinner.

Papa's gone for five minutes, then ten minutes. My stomach is really growling now, so I get up from the couch and go upstairs to their bedroom. Maybe I can say hi to Auntie Lillian on the phone. She and Mama always talk for a long time whenever she calls.

Their bedroom door is shut, which is different, but I can still hear their voices, or at least, sort of. They're a little muffled. I press my ear to the door the way I sometimes see people do in movies when they want to hear through closed doors. It usually works for them. I probably shouldn't be doing this, because when the people in movies listen at doors, they shouldn't be either, but I can't stop myself. Plus, I'm hungry, I need to know if they're coming back out soon so we can eat.

"He seemed fine a few days ago when Lillian and I saw him," Mama says. Her voice is quiet, but in a different way than it is when she's trying to make sure we both use our inside voices. "I'm just so shocked, I guess that's all."

"I know. I'm sorry." Papa's voice, too, is a different quiet than usual. Serious. Maybe his work voice. "What are you going to do next?"

"Tell Charlotte, I guess." Mama sounds tired, but I have to keep listening, because she's talking about me now. "She was going to have to learn about death eventually."

"You think she'll be okay?"

"I'd rather tell her than hide it, don't you think?"

I frown. I think I know what death is, but it only happens to bad characters in movies. Like Jafar in *Aladdin*, or Mother Gothel in *Tangled,* or the Emperor in *Star Wars*. Some good characters die, like Mufasa in *The Lion King*, but he gets to come back as a ghost and talk to Simba, so I don't consider him to be completely dead. Good characters always get to come back somehow. They're never really gone.

"How do we tell her?" Papa, too, sounds tired now.

"We just let her ask questions." Mama's voice has gone soft, a gentle soft, but I can hear something sad in it. "And we answer them as best we can. We can't shelter her from everything forever."

"Before or after dinner?"

"After. I want to make sure she eats." The bed creaks. Mama's softer footsteps head for the bedroom door.

I jump up off the floor like I've been shocked and run back down the stairs, trying to keep my footsteps as quiet as possible as I launch myself back on to the couch and try to pretend I've been there all along. I throw my feet up on the armrest like I sometimes see Papa do when he's reading and fold my shirt at the edge, but all I can think about is what Mama and Papa are going to tell me when dinner's done. There's a funny feeling in my stomach.

"Hi, sweetie," Mama says, and I turn to look at her as she comes into the living room, her dark hair pulled back into a high ponytail on top of her head. Her face is a little red, and the corners of her mouth look sad. "Sorry we took so long. Let's eat, I bet you're hungry."

"Mama, did someone die?"

I'm not sure why I suddenly ask the question, but I know I don't want to wait until after dinner to hear the answer. The funny feeling in my stomach is suddenly a lot stronger, like hundreds of birds all taking off at the same time.

I watch Mama's face for her reaction. Her face is very still, a little scared almost, and behind her, Papa looks shocked. Nervous, even. Why are they nervous? I know what death is.

Finally, Mama says, "Yes, sweetie, it was Grandpa." Her voice is quiet, maybe hesitating, as though she's waiting for me to explode.

"Did he do something bad?"

"What?"

"Only the bad characters die, right?"

"Ah." Mama approaches the couch now, takes a seat next to me, and I take my feet off the armrest and sit with my legs crossed to look at her. "No, honey, Grandpa was a really good man. A lot of times, really good people have to die, too. It happens to everyone, especially when they get old."

"Was Grandpa old?"

A pause. "He was seventy-two."

"Is that old?"

Another pause. "It's pretty old, sweetie."

"Okay." I'm frowning, because I'm still not sure why Grandpa has to die when he isn't a bad character in my story. Whenever we visited him, he always brought me a coloring book and took me out for ice cream, and he always let me get extra sprinkles. He would tell me how much he loves my drawings and that I'm going to be an artist someday.

Sometimes Grandpa would tell me stories about Mama when she was little. When she was little, they lived just outside Toronto, only an hour away from where we live now, which is ten minutes away from the middle of the city. It's always funny to hear about how Mama used to do things I do now, like draw pictures in the dirt with a stick or try and jump off the swing at its highest point. Sometimes he would show me pictures of Mama from when she was little. There aren't very many—she's in the middle of four siblings—but I like seeing how much I look like her when she was my age. It's that little reminder that I come from her.

I look at Mama now, waiting for me to say something, so I ask. "But that means he'll come back, right?"

A pause. "What do you mean, sweetie?"

"Like Mufasa." I stop, trying to figure out the words. "You know, like how he came back to talk to Simba. He was a good character. He comes back, so all the good ones get to come back, right?"

Mama draws a long breath, and I can see the smallest twitch in her face. Later, when I'm older, I will realize that is the moment when her composure threatened to slip, when it truly sank in for her that he will not come back and she will have to be the one to tell me so.

"Charlotte, sweetie." Mama reaches for my hand. "You won't get to see Grandpa again. In the real world, they don't come back." She breathes out, slowly. Squeezes my hand. "But that's okay. He'll stay with us because we'll remember him, right?"

"Of course we will." I nod. I'm frowning because I think she's wrong. I think I can see Grandpa again in this world, if I really try hard enough to talk to him, because I think he would come out from the silver mist for me like Mufasa does for Simba. He can point me in the right direction.

"Sweetie, are you okay?"

I turn to look at Mama again and shrug. "Yeah, I guess so."

\*\*\*

Mama and Papa always talk to me after dinner. That's our time for the three of us. After I help one of them with the dishes, Papa sits down on the couch with a glass of wine and Mama brings out a little bit of cake and we talk about anything. I show them my drawings, or we talk about what I did in school if it's during the school year, or we talk about what I did at camp if I'm doing a camp that week. When it's time for bed, Papa will ask me what I want for lunch and pack it for me if I'm going to camp or school, or he'll leave it in a place I can reach in the fridge.

After Grandpa dies, Mama shuts herself in their room after every dinner. I help Papa with the dishes, and he takes a bottle of wine up to their closed bedroom door.

I arrange my lunch for the next day, straining to reach the food I want from the top shelf. When I go upstairs to my room, I draw pictures of Mama in the dark in her bedroom and Papa with his arm around her, the bottle of wine in between them. I draw pictures of Grandpa pushing me on the swing or Grandpa emerging from the mist as Mufasa.

At 8:30, when it's time to go to bed, I tuck myself in and wait for Mama to come say goodnight. When she does, she's in and out of the room really fast. Her face is wet, and her eyes are sad.

When she leaves, I cry myself to sleep, but I don't really know why. I just know that I keep waiting for Grandpa to emerge from the stars or the mist to talk to me, and he never shows up.

\*\*\*

Once, two years ago, when Grandpa still drove close to the city to visit us instead of the other way around, he helped me draw a castle in the dirt and imagine the whole world around it. The castle had six towers, and flying dragons and winged horses swooped around it. The kingdom had an army of a hundred thousand men. Grandpa was the king and I was the queen, and he said I got to be in charge because he was much too old to be making those kinds of important decisions when he knew I could do it.

"You know what to do, Charlotte," he said. "What's the most important thing for everyone in your kingdom?"

It takes me a second to remember, because Grandpa has asked me this question before but not about the kingdom. *"What's the most important thing for everyone in our family?"*

"That they have everything they need and that they feel love," I said.

"Good girl." Grandpa patted me on the head. "You'll be the queen of a real kingdom one day."

I smiled up at him. His eyes twinkled down at me behind wire-framed glasses, a gentle smile on his face that reminds me of Mama's. "I know," I said.

Grandpa's smile widened. "Stay right there a second. Keep an eye on the castle. I'm going to get something, I'll be right back."

Even two years ago, his footsteps were starting to slow down. His feet shuffled when he walked, and I watched him go into the house and grab something off the table. When he came back out, I saw him holding up the camera. He always brought his camera when he came to visit—to make sure to keep memories, he said. When we started driving to visit him instead, he always asked for the camera, and he always took at least one picture of me each time.

Grandpa came back out of the house with the strap of the camera around his wrist. The camera sang, and the lens popped out.

"Smile, Charlotte," he said, when he got close enough and held out the camera for me to look into, and I did, sitting in the dirt next to the castle we'd drawn and the kingdom we'd built around it. There was that soft clicking sound that I loved from every time he took a picture. As he checked the little screen on the back, his smile became more gentle, and the lines around his eyes crinkled. "That's a keeper for sure."

***

A lot of people start coming over to our house, and I don't always know who they are, but they always bring food. Auntie Lillian begins coming over to the house two days after Mama starts hiding in her room after dinner. Usually, she convinces Mama to come out and sit downstairs in the living room. When I'm drawing in the kitchen after dinner, I hear them talking about what suit Grandpa will wear, what they plan to say about him, the best way to go about dividing

Grandpa's money and other things between the four siblings. I don't see why they can't just divide everything evenly. That's what I think Grandpa would want anyway. Plus, I learned in school how important sharing is.

I go with them to his house before the funeral, when they go through his clothes to pick out the suit. Mama asked me if I wanted to stay with Papa, but I wanted to come to Grandpa's house in case he might come out of the fog around there. Maybe it's just that we're too far, and he can't see into my house.

While Mama and her three siblings argue over which color tie would be best, I wander downstairs into Grandpa's study. I wonder, a little bit, if Grandpa will be sitting in the big chair on the other side of the desk the way he was sometimes when Mama and I would show up to surprise him. The chair is empty, but at a slight angle, as if he's just gotten up and will be back any second.

I step around the desk and climb into the chair. I sink far down into the leather, too far down to use the desk, but I feel like Grandpa, for a second. The chair smells like wood smoke, probably because of the fireplace across from the desk, and like newspapers and coffee. His hugs smelled like that, too.

Grandpa has lots of photos on his desk, all in a row along the top. I recognize Mama from when she was younger, her brown hair loose and almost to her stomach, and Auntie Lillian with her brown hair in a long ponytail. There's a picture of Grandpa and who I think is Grandma together, but I don't remember meeting Grandma before she died.

The floor creaks outside, and I should get up from the chair, but instead, I stay put when Mama puts her head around the door. "Charlotte?"

When she sees me in Grandpa's chair, she freezes, and I watch her draw a long breath before fixing a small smile on to her face. "How are you doing, sweetie?"

"Who's going to take pictures if Grandpa isn't here?"

A pause. Another long breath. "We'll make sure to take lots of pictures."

I nod. "Okay."

"You know," Mama says, her voice soft and watery, "Grandpa said you could keep the camera."

My eyes get big. "Really?"

"Yes." Mama smiles, and this time, she doesn't have to fix it on to her face. "Just be really careful with it, okay? It's your last gift from Grandpa."

"When can I have it?"

"I'll bring it to you when I find it."

"Promise?"

"Promise. Are you okay here?"

"Yeah." I look back at the row of photos on top of Grandpa's desk and see the one of myself, sitting in the dirt next to the picture of our castle and our kingdom and our hundred-thousand-man army. I can almost see Grandpa standing behind the camera, smiling as he takes the picture. "I'm okay here, Mama."

"Okay." Mama's smile twists slightly to one side, and before I can figure out what it is or why she did it, she's turned around and left the room.

I stay in the chair, wondering if I'll hear Grandpa come around the corner to surprise me for a change.

***

Everyone cries at a funeral. That's what I discover, seven days after Grandpa dies. Even Papa is crying, which makes me nervous because Papa doesn't cry, ever. I cry, too, but I think it's because Mama is crying, and I hate it when Mama cries because something has to be really bad for Mama to cry.

There is a big picture of Grandpa from when he was a little younger, and I can't stop looking at it, because even though we're all crying about the fact that he's gone, I sort of wonder if he's still here. It's foggy today, and I'm still hoping Grandpa will find his way out of it to talk to me.

Once we come home, I change into pajamas and sit on my bed and draw another picture of Grandpa coming out of the fog. I'm having a hard time getting his eyes exactly right when there's a soft knock on my door and Mama pushes it open without warning.

"Charlotte," she says, coming to sit on my bed, and I flip the paper over because I don't want her to see what I'm doing in case it makes her sad all over again. She isn't looking at my paper, though; she's holding something in her hands. I recognize the case for Grandpa's camera, and my heart beats a little bit faster.

Mama holds the camera out to me. "Be careful with it, sweetie, okay?"

I take it with extra delicate hands, so she knows how careful I'm going to be with it. "I'll be careful."

That night, I put the camera under my pillow before I go to sleep. It has so many of Grandpa's memories in it. I have to protect it.

\*\*\*

Sometimes, I hear Mama crying in her bedroom, right after she picks me up from camp, but Papa isn't always home to put his arm around her the way he does when she gets scared or sad during movies because he comes back from work right before dinner. So after I get some food for an afternoon snack, I go to my room and hold the camera in my lap and I cry, too, because I can't make Mama stop crying. I want to ask Grandpa a million questions, but he still hasn't come to talk to me, so I can't even ask him when he's coming back.

\*\*\*

Mama still calls me for dinner every day at six. When I tell her my stories from camp or talk about my drawings, she smiles and asks me about what's going to happen tomorrow. Papa pours a glass of wine for both of them, and we sit together in the living room. I draw pictures of Grandpa or of the squirrel I saw running around in the backyard.

Mama doesn't always go right to her room after her dinner, not anymore, but she still does sometimes. She always comes back out to say goodnight.

\*\*\*

One day, three weeks after Grandpa dies, I run up to my room and grab the camera. I can hear Mama and Papa talking downstairs, but I have an idea as I'm remembering all my good times with Grandpa.

"Why do you always take pictures, Grandpa?" I always asked. I knew the answer, but I liked hearing him say it because of the way his eyes would crinkle when he looked down at me to tell me.

*"To make sure to keep the memories, Charlotte,"* he always said.

*"How do you know which ones to keep? What if some of the pictures aren't good?"*

*"Just because the picture isn't good doesn't mean it isn't a good memory, don't you think?"*

I sit down on the floor of my bedroom with the camera and find the on/off button. It takes a second, because I'm used to mostly watching Grandpa do it, but the camera sings as I turn it on, just like it did for Grandpa.

I run back downstairs with the camera in hand, the strap securely around my wrist the way Grandpa would always hold it. My socks slide a little on the wooden floor right when I stop running, and Mama and Papa both raise their eyebrows when they see me. Mama is smiling, a little, and Papa looks confused.

"Smile!" I say, and I hold the camera up and push the big round button. The camera makes that soft clicking noise I love, and I check the little screen on the back. Mama and Papa are smiling, a little confused, but everyone always smiles right away whenever someone holds up a camera.

"What are you doing, Charlotte?" Mama asks.

"Making sure to keep the memories," I say, smiling at her over the top of the camera.

"Is that Grandpa's?" Papa asks.

I nod, excited, and Mama's smile softens around the edges. "Good job, Charlotte."

For a moment, I almost think I hear Grandpa's low rumbly voice, but when I strain my ears to listen for it, it's gone again.

\*\*\*

Eventually, after two more months go by, Mama stops disappearing into her room after dinner, and a big picture of Grandpa appears over our fireplace. She puts up the picture of me next to my castle in the dirt, too, even though I'm five in that picture and I'm seven now. Auntie Lillian comes over every once in a while, and sometimes, I take a picture of her with Grandpa's camera. Papa shows me how to move the pictures from the camera over to the computer so that there's room on the memory card for more memories.

Mama doesn't cry as much anymore, so I don't, either. I keep sleeping with the camera under my pillow every night, because I don't want to forget to make memories the way Grandpa asked me to. I'm still waiting for him to come out of the stars or the fog to talk to me. Good characters always come back somehow, for the people they love to see them so they can talk to each other about important things.

I want to ask him what he thinks of the memories I'm keeping. I want to know if he thinks they're good memories, too.

2.

# WHAT ARE WORDS

*Carolyn, 26, New York City, 2017*
*"I always thought I knew who you were."*

"This feels wrong."

Carolyn Garnet stands in the doorway of her mother's bedroom, arms folded, chewing on her lower lip. The sheets on the bed are slightly rumpled, one corner of the comforter tossed back. A sweater and a pair of jeans hang over the back of the desk chair. One of the curtains is pulled back slightly, letting in a sliver of sunlight that warms a patch on the wooden floor even though it is winter in New York City and everything is gray, sharp, and cold. Everything about the room is waiting—waiting for Skylar Garnet to return when, in fact, she never will.

A gentle hand lands on Carolyn's shoulder, and she turns her face up to look at her older brother. Josh's expression is serious, carefully controlled, but Carolyn can see the sadness behind his hazel eyes. Still, he's the one who asks, "You okay?"

"I don't know yet." Carolyn worries, a little, that because she hasn't cried much at all, it means somehow that she didn't love her mother, even though she knows that's stupid. Of course, she loved her mother. "I guess so."

"I'm proud of you." Josh tries to ruffle her hair, and Carolyn ducks out of the way and into her mother's bedroom, over to the desk in the corner.

"Tell Alex he needs to get here soon, or I'm taking everything Mom left for him in the will," Carolyn says. "I'm only sort of kidding."

"Ouch." Alex steps into the room, and Carolyn gives her oldest brother a sheepish grin. For a moment, this feels normal, all three of them together back in the house where they grew up. But then Carolyn remembers that she just made a joke using her mother's death, and it reminds her that her mother is really gone. The grin fades from her face as she turns back to the desk and pulls a stack of books out of the left cabinet. "I didn't know Mom kept so much stuff. I don't think I've ever seen any of these books before in my life."

"Explains where I got my hoarding tendencies from." Alex laughs, but it hangs in the air, awkward.

Carolyn hauls a small box out of the back of the cabinet. It's heavy, so it must be books. She's right. They're all identical, small purple notebooks. Twelve of them. "Do you guys know what these are?"

Josh comes up behind her, lifts the top one off the stack, and flips back the cover. "I guess Mom kept journals."

"Really? I didn't know that." Alex comes up behind Carolyn and reaches for one. "When do they start?"

Carolyn reaches for the notebook at the top of the stack, flips through a few pages, catches her own name, and starts to read properly. "Oh, wow. I didn't know she kept journals. Wait, this is so exciting, I want to look at them now."

"Did she say what to do with any writing we found?" Josh picks up another notebook to thumb through.

"Trash it, right?" Alex says. "I think that's what her will says."

"Yeah." Carolyn places the notebook back into the box and sets the lid back on, but a frown tugs at her eyebrows. "I'll get rid of them."

Instead, Carolyn takes them to her own bedroom and stacks them all on her desk to read later. She figures it might be nice to keep them around for a bit and peek at what her mother said about having Alex, Josh, and herself. Skylar Garnet was such a sparkling person that Carolyn feels her words, too, have to have that same indescribable sparkle, that glow that draws everyone in. Maybe her mother's words can help her write her eulogy.

\*\*\*

Five days later, seated in the front row of guests at the funeral home only a few blocks away, Carolyn smooths her hand over the papers containing the words she'd agonized over and rewritten more than six times in those five days. Josh is wrapping up his eulogy, his words drifting in the room around her and coming to rest on her shoulders. The burden of expectation, she supposes.

When Josh introduces her, Carolyn steps up to the podium to speak, her breath rattling in her throat and a sour taste on her tongue as a purple notebook deep in the pocket of her black jumpsuit shifts and pokes her in the thigh with each step.

\*\*\*

"Before I dive in, I'd like to thank you all for coming out to celebrate my mother's life. For those of you I haven't had the pleasure of meeting, I'm Carolyn Garnet, Skylar's daughter.

"When I was writing this, I knew she wanted to make sure I'd forgo the—quote—'boring details' of her life, but I want to tell them to you anyways, because there is nothing about her life that isn't remarkable to me. She was born Skylar Hawkins on November 12, 1958, the only girl in a family with four boys. She was a CEO, an entrepreneur, a philanthropist who raised thousands of dollars. But even with all these accomplishments to her name, to me, she was Mom.

"I spent a long time working on this, trying to figure out the best story to tell that would capture my mom. The perfect moment. I thought about all those times she crushed me at badminton even after she taught me all her tricks. They make for pretty good stories, but there are too many of them—although there was that one time she managed to clock me in the face with a birdie. I had a bruise on my cheek for a week. She was so embarrassed about that; she would apologize every time I brought it up. I never let her live that down."

Carolyn allows herself a glance at her audience and then wonders why she did. The faces blend together for her; only Josh and Alex stand out. And they are waiting for her to keep going.

"I thought about telling a story from the trip my family took after my college graduation—we went to Thailand because we'd never been and Mom had always wanted to go—and on one of the first days, when everyone else was down from the jetlag at 1 PM, Mom took me on a spontaneous trip to the Temple of the Dawn. She goes, 'Hey. I'm bored. You want to go sightseeing?' and it was one of those moments where I had a choice, but I didn't have a choice. Yeah, Josh, I see you laughing. He knows those moments with my mother."

Carolyn meets his gaze and lets herself smile, just for a little.

"We took a taxi all the way to the river—it took us thirty minutes with traffic—and a boat up the river to the temple. We're as white as they come, and we don't speak a single word of Thai, but Mom took charge anyway. You know that nervous feeling you get when one of your friends says, 'Don't worry, I got this,' and then they walk away and you feel like you're at the controls of a runaway train but the train is sentient and you can almost feel the energy humming under your feet and all around you? That's what it was like around my mother, all the time."

Carolyn's voice falters as she adjusts her stance behind the podium, feels the purple notebook poke her in the thigh through her jumpsuit pocket. She glances up through her eyelashes and locks eyes with Josh, who offers her a tiny smile.

Carolyn draws a sharp breath and smooths her hand over the paper.

"One minute she's asking someone on a street corner for directions to the dock, and the next minute, somehow, I had a ticket in my hand and we were on the riverboat, but I really had and still have no idea how we got there. She was not at all afraid to walk up to people and ask questions if it meant she could get to where she wanted to go. She was very nice about it. She always said, 'Excuse me,' or 'Could you help me?' but as someone who wanted to avoid being seen as the stereotypical loud American tourist, it was a little embarrassing. But it was also one hundred percent worth it even in all that heat and humidity to finally get there and see that ornate architecture gleaming all around us.

"That story seemed right. It captures Mom in her element, abuzz with an adventure, eager to move and keep moving. I've got other ones—spontaneous ski trips to Utah or Colorado, late nights watching the Olympics so she can see if her badminton bracket will hold up, that one time Alex and I came home from just a regular day at school to find her in the middle of replacing all the curtains in the house because she freaked out and realized that none of them matched the aesthetics of the rooms they were in. Alex, I see you laughing. We talk about that day a lot. It's a trademark Skylar Garnet moment."

Now, when Carolyn looks up, faces are starting to come into focus. Faces nodding up and down, with a faint smile here and there. Lost in their recollections of her mother.

"But all those stories I have of Mom bouncing off the walls, running around to get things done, making sure she was busy and her three kids and her husband were busier—they leave out the beautiful quiet moments she could have, too. And because they were few and far between, because they didn't last very long, we always knew they were valuable when we got them.

"A couple of months ago, Mom came to visit me at my apartment, which she did every week. She brought me a plaid blanket scarf. No special occasion, but that's Mom, bringing an unexpected gift when she feels like it. She handed me the scarf wrapped in tissue paper, the whole thing taped together with a silver sticker. Not my birthday, not an anniversary, not a special holiday. Just because she wanted to. I would always tell her, 'Thanks, I don't need it, but I really appreciate it.' And she would always say, 'I know that, Carolyn. But you know how much I like getting you things.' Gift-giving. It was always Mom's love language. This time, she also said, 'It brings out the highlights in your hair. Perfect for fall.' And when I protested, because I have dozens of scarves already, she patted my hand, smiled, and said, 'Please. It's a gift.'

"It wasn't a big revelation or anything. No crumbling or rebuilding of our relationship, no bombshell or long-kept secret dropped. Just one of those tiny quiet moments, mother to daughter, where I looked at her face and saw the love in her eyes. That sparkle, the laughter lines, that bright smile that never changed. And that moment, too, is a trademark Skylar Garnet moment. Looking at her and seeing how much love, how much warmth radiates off her when she looks at you. At anyone."

Carolyn stares at the words on the page. She wonders, like she did when she was writing, if those quiet moments meant something different to her mother than they did to her. But her audience is waiting.

"I came to realize that there is no one moment I can point to that captures everything about my mother. She was always sparkling, humming with energy, always ready for a spontaneous adventure. She was a giver. Of gifts, love, everything and anything you could imagine. And I'll really miss her. Mom, I hope you're still sparkling up there."

Carolyn flips the page over as soft applause rings through the room. For a moment, she can see that look of love on her mother's face she just described. She's been on the receiving end of it many times. But as she steps down from the podium and folds the pages into her pocket, her fingers brush against that damn purple notebook, and a fist closes around her heart, squeezing doubt into it.

***

Carolyn dips into the funeral home's kitchen to breathe, away from the crush of people who will undoubtedly want to compliment her words about her mother. She's not sure she can muster the energy to keep shining the spotlight. The words she spoke were words she knows she still believes, but the sour taste on her tongue and the purple notebook in her pocket are twisting her thoughts.

Instead of the space she wants, Carolyn finds herself crushed in a tight hug between Alex, who's six-foot-five, and Josh, who's six-foot-two. At five-foot-seven, she's used to being the tall one around her friends at school, but she doesn't mind being the short one around Alex and Josh, even in three-inch heels. Whether she's twelve or twenty-six, they make her feel safe.

"Great job, Caro," Alex says, and Carolyn can feel her oldest brother's deep voice rumbling in his chest against her ear. "Mom would have really liked that."

"Maybe." Carolyn isn't so sure. She's not sure Alex would be, either, if he knew what Mom had said about Carolyn, but he doesn't know she kept the journals against their mother's will, read her words after they discovered them in the back of the left cabinet on Mom's desk. She misses only knowing the Mom who would come into her room with a snack and hot tea when she was up late studying. It was much more straightforward.

Carolyn keeps her arms around her brother, holding him for just a little bit longer. She doesn't get to see him as often as she'd like to even though she knows it's the nature of adulthood, that they either have to schedule time for one another or are brought together because of a funeral. "I hope she did," she says.

"She did. You know she did." Josh musses her hair, and Carolyn swats him, trying to get his arm. Josh ducks away, grinning, and for a moment, the air around them loosens as Carolyn smooths her hair back down and gives him a glare that's betrayed by the slight smile tugging at the corners of her mouth. For a moment, she is thirteen and Josh is seventeen, and Mom is still here, telling him to leave his sister alone and throwing a wink Carolyn's way to let her know that she's on her side.

But Carolyn remembers that little purple notebook shoved in one of the deep pockets of her jumpsuit, and the pit in her stomach curdles, growing hot.

\*\*\*

Josh's grin softens and fades as he watches Carolyn's face change, but she shakes her head when he gives her a questioning look. She turns away, draws a breath, and straightens her shoulders. "I'd better go check on the food that's out there already and make sure people haven't gotten in a fight."

"No one gets in a fight at a funeral," Alex says.

"You never know." Josh winks at his older brother.

"Guys, stop." Josh can hear Carolyn's voice rising, but his little sister disappears before either Josh or Alex can stop her.

"She needs to slow down," Alex says. "She's going to burn out."

"She'll slow down after this is over," Josh says, but Alex is right. Carolyn has been moving nonstop since Mom died. Apart from the decisions the three of them made together—the location, what Mom should wear, where she should be buried, and a few legal things they'd all had to go over together—Carolyn did everything, a responsibility that had been left to Mom when Dad died. She'd sent the invites, booked the location, organized the caterer. She hasn't stopped running since the week started.

"Check in on her," Alex says, clapping Josh on the shoulder. "And like, really check in on her, make sure she's okay."

"What, you can't do it?" Josh asks, teasing. "I'm kidding, I swear."

Alex shrugs. "You guys have always been closer. Just the age thing." Two years separate Alex from Josh and four years separate Josh from Carolyn. Alex had already graduated college by the time Carolyn started. But they both know it's more than that. Alex takes after their father, with his dark brown hair and eyes and his absurd knack for logic problems, but Josh and Carolyn share the same light red hair, the same hazel eyes. They share an optimistic outlook on life and a methodical approach to study, even though Carolyn is the biologist and Josh is the artist. When Alex went to college, Josh had just gotten his license, so he became Carolyn's ride to and from school, and they began to talk, every morning and afternoon.

Now, Josh holds his hands up. "I know, I know. I'll check in on her."

Alex nods, and silence hangs in the air between them before Josh decides to ask. "You good?"

Alex shrugs, exhales, and the mask of the smooth-talking entrepreneur, the one who has it all together, slides a little bit. "Not great. But it'll get better. You?"

Josh shrugs. "I don't know." He doesn't know if he's more worried about Carolyn or still trying to figure himself out. "But you're right. It will get better."

"Yeah." Alex hugs Josh, and for a moment, they are just two brothers like they usually are, not the two sons of their mother who has just passed away.

But then Alex steps back and adjusts his suit jacket as he starts toward the kitchen door. "We better not hide for too long. People will come looking." He melts back into the crowded room inside before Josh has a chance to answer.

\*\*\*

"Beautiful words earlier, Carolyn. Loved hearing that story about Thailand from your side."

"Your mother is so proud, looking down from up there. I bet your father is too."

"Such a touching tribute you gave up there. And so well-spoken."

Each time, Carolyn shakes a hand, gives a hug, and thanks the person for coming, for their condolences. Faces begin to blend, even though this is a small gathering, as far as funerals go. Before arriving at the funeral home today, she hadn't met all of her mother's extended family, all of her mother's friends who are now here.

Carolyn wants to sit down, but if she sits down, someone will compliment her on her eulogy again and then because she will be seated and can be cornered, they will ask her how she's doing, and she doesn't want to answer that question. If she's still for too long, the pit that's been in her stomach for a week now will catch fire, that fist around her heart will squeeze ever tighter, and she will lose her temper at her mother's funeral.

Carolyn squeezes between Mom's best friend Lori talking with Mom's brother Zach and the wall that leads to the kitchen door. She needs to check on the caterer and see if he needs a break.

"Hey, whoa, slow down." A gentle hand grabs her wrist, pulls her out of the crowd, and up by a window that's been cracked open. "Deep breaths, Caro."

She knows it's Josh from the fact that he's the only one here who would pull her out of that crowd to take a minute for herself. "Josh, I need to check on the caterer."

"Alex is around, he knows what you've set up, he can take care of things if there's a real emergency." Josh's voice is soft, but Carolyn hears that firm edge, the one she's known not to argue with since she was a teenager. "Come on. Just step out for a minute."

Carolyn runs a hand through her light red hair as her brother pushes open the back door to the funeral home. It's mid-December in New York City, the wind cold and sharp as it hits her face, but she and Josh are alone, even if it's just for a minute. She leans on the railing of the stairs and lets a long breath unfurl into the air like candle smoke. Is this when she's supposed to cry? She hasn't yet, not at the funeral, anyways, but she's put it down to the fear of having to stand up in front of all her relatives and Mom's friends and deliver the eulogy she'd agonized over for days because the words she'd wanted to say about Mom had become clouded, but she still needed to believe in the Mom she knew.

Josh leans against the railing, arms folded over his chest. "Go ahead. Say whatever."

Carolyn smiles, and for a heartbeat, her anger cools. Josh knows she hates the *"How are you doing?"* question, so this is his way of asking. It has been, for years. "Honestly? Fuck all of this. I'm so tired. I don't want any of this. We shouldn't be here."

"Yeah." Josh raises his eyebrows and puffs a short sigh. "Honestly."

Carolyn folds her arms over her chest and wishes she'd grabbed a jacket. The sharp New York wind that had nipped at her face in welcome is starting to hurt. "Your turn. Say whatever."

"I don't know." Josh throws a hand up, then lets it fall to his side. "It's all just so… surreal."

"Yeah." Carolyn's voice comes out softer than she intended. "You gave a great tribute, by the way." She hates that she's giving him this compliment because she doesn't feel the same about her words, but she means it for Josh. His eulogy was centered on their mother's love of words and the fact that there was not one word that could accurately describe her. Josh always had a knack for poetic language. His eulogy reminded her of a song, unburdened by their mother's own words.

Josh gives her his usual crooked smile. "Yeah, thanks."

"No, I really mean it." Carolyn tilts her head to one side.

Josh's smile softens. "Yeah, I know. Thanks, Caro." He scuffs at the concrete with one foot and straightens up from leaning on the rail. "I promise yours was good too. I know you were worried about it."

Carolyn fights the urge to roll her eyes as she brushes down her jumpsuit even though it's spotless. She needs to make Josh understand the reason she had to show him and Alex three different versions, why she was rewriting it till the day before the funeral. "You know the reason my eulogy was so hard to write?"

Josh stills instantly. Carolyn can feel his eyes on her, and she wants to turn around. Stop whatever's about to come out of her mouth. But she's already started. She's been carrying this with her, because she knows her frustrations aren't directed just at her mother but also at herself. Her ears are getting hot, a sure sign that she's going to lose her temper, and she draws a long breath.

"Remember when we were going through Mom's room, and we found her journals?" It's a rhetorical question. Carolyn knows he remembers. "I actually kept them."

Josh's eyebrows go up. "Yeah? Why?"

"I don't know." Carolyn has been trying to justify that to herself all week. "I missed her, I guess. She never said she kept journals so she never said we couldn't read them. And I guess I thought… I thought reading her words would be like hearing her voice, like having her around again."

Josh smiles. "Now you sound like me."

"Shut up." Carolyn rolls her eyes, but she appreciates Josh lightening the moment for her. He's always been good at that. "I was reading through the last one, the most recent one." Carolyn picks at the pocket holding the little purple notebook, and the pit in her stomach flares red-hot. "Can I read you something?"

Josh's eyes widen as she pulls the notebook out of her pocket. She opens it to the page she's marked with the purple ribbon as the knot in her stomach twists, pulls tighter, and doubt oozes out of her heart and into her veins, bringing it right back.

***

The second Carolyn pulls the purple notebook out of her pocket, Josh's stomach sinks. When he and Caro had pulled out the big box of notebooks from the bottom cabinet of Mom's desk, he'd felt cautious. Nervous, even, as Carolyn had pulled back the lid of the box and gotten excited about finding her words, over thirty years of their mother's life documented in front of them. Skylar Garnet had been a force to be reckoned with in a public space. Her private words could probably blow someone to bits.

Josh watches as Carolyn flips to a page marked by a purple ribbon. She's been saving it for a moment like this, and that makes him uneasy.

Carolyn meets Josh's eye and then drops her gaze to the page.

"'I'm hoping I can convince Carolyn it's time to get a move on and really push toward med school. I know she's been saving and applying, but she's twenty-six, it's about time she gave a real big push. She can't be lazy; that goes against the Hawkins name, even if she doesn't carry it. I've tried to talk to her about it, make sure she has goals she's working toward, but she always seems to shut down whenever I ask her about what she's pushing for in her career. Makes me think she doesn't have any goals, any direction, and that she's going to get stuck here forever with nothing to aim for. The boys have done so much already—Alex is married and well on the way with his startup, Josh is doing so well with his writing, and he's with Diego now—and I don't want Carolyn to fall behind them and bring the Hawkins family standard down with her.'"

The notebook snaps shut. "Can you believe that?"

"Oh, come on, Caro, she's just saying those things because she's worried. And I'll bet she never thought you'd ever get your hands on them." Josh holds a hand up as Carolyn opens her mouth. "Hang on, I'm not done. I know that hurts. I know it sucks to read those things about yourself. But it's coming from a place of love. I promise it is."

Carolyn runs a hand through her hair, and the light red strands settle at her shoulders as she paces back and forth on the tiny stoop. "That's one of the last entries. She died thinking I'm lazy and I'm going to let down the family name because I'm not going to go anywhere in life. I'm not lazy. I've been applying to med schools since I graduated. I've been working at the lab to make sure I can pay for med school without going into hundreds of thousands of dollars of debt. I don't know what she wants from me."

"Carolyn, look at me," Josh says, his voice sharp, and Carolyn stops and runs a hand through her hair again. Josh can see the four-year-old behind her eyes, the little girl needing to know whether Santa Claus is real because if he isn't, everything will change. "Why do you think she's saying those things?"

"Because I was letting down her expectations? Because she truly didn't think I could achieve anything without someone holding my hand the whole way?" Carolyn folds her arms over her chest. "Do you want me to keep going? Because I can."

"Carolyn." Josh puffs a sigh of frustration. He knows their mother loved Carolyn, that she was proud of her, but it's his word against the words on the page. "She had high expectations for you because that's the Hawkins family standard and the Garnet family standard. We dream big and we achieve bigger. You are the youngest of three, and you're the only girl, in true Hawkins family tradition. Of course, she's going to pin a lot on you. So much was pinned on her, remember? The only girl surrounded by four brothers? You know she had to work hard to keep up with them. Harder, even. The glass ceiling was higher then than it is now."

Josh watches the tight expression on Carolyn's face waver.

"She just saw herself in you. That's what's behind that." Josh slides his hands in his suit pockets. "I can't prove it to you, but I know that's what it is."

"No, I know that." Carolyn tips her head back, looks up at the sky, and breathes out. When she speaks again, Josh can hear the heat in it, that flaming temper she's always fought to control. "It's just I always felt she supported me no matter what, you know? Like even when I would bring home a bad grade or break one of her grandma's plates. She always forgave me once she made sure I'd learned from my mistake. But when I read that, everything changed. And I hated delivering that eulogy knowing she'd said and thought all of those things about me. That I'm going to end up being less than you guys. A let-down."

"You're not. Look at me." Josh takes a step forward; the movement pulls Carolyn's eyes to him. "You are exactly where you need to be, and that is perfect for all of us. Including Mom. You believe those things you said in your eulogy, don't you? About those quiet moments, the love we could always see?"

"Yes." Her instant response makes Josh feel better.

"Then that's what matters." Josh leans back against the railing. "Did she try to talk to you about it?"

"Yes," Carolyn says, and Josh raises his eyebrows, but she keeps going. "And I did always shut down, but it was because I couldn't deal with her telling me that I needed to speed up and make sure I got on track for success as soon as possible. It's too much pressure. I want to go at my own pace and tell her when the good things happened."

"I think she might have seen that as you not wanting to tell her that you were failing." Josh holds his hand up as Carolyn's brows pull together and she opens her mouth. "I'm not saying you were failing. I'm just saying that to her, the fact that you didn't look like you were making progress meant that you were stagnant, so it seemed like you hadn't succeeded."

Carolyn's expression loosens a little, and her eyes turn upward and to the right. "I should have talked to her." Her eyes stay averted.

"You won't have that chance."

"I know."

"She can still see you. I know she can." Josh allows himself to smile a little, and Carolyn's slight smile tugs the corners of her mouth. "She loves you. She knows you have so much potential. And maybe that's why she was hard on you. It was just miscommunication, you know?"

When Carolyn bites her lip, wavering, Josh adds, "At worst, take them as fighting words. Use them to fuel yourself. Prove her wrong. Just don't lose sight of the good things."

Carolyn draws a long breath and squares her shoulders. "Okay."

For some reason, Josh wants to laugh, maybe because it's a classic Carolyn-Josh interaction. He knows she's thinking about what he's said, though, so he says nothing else and instead crushes her in a hug.

"Careful, I've got makeup on," Carolyn says, muffled against his suit jacket. "Wouldn't want to ruin your suit."

"Wouldn't want to ruin your makeup, more like," Josh says, ruffling her hair, but he steps back anyway and grins at her as she scowls and swats at him. "I'm kidding. I appreciate it. This is an expensive suit."

"It's nice." Carolyn pulls open the funeral home door and steps back inside. She's already transformed back into her efficient self. Always on the go. Just like Skylar Garnet, Josh realizes, as he follows her back into the chatter.

\*\*\*

An hour and a half later, Carolyn closes the front door of their house behind her and sinks down on the couch next to Josh. "Jesus, I'm exhausted."

"Gee, I wonder why," Alex says from the kitchen, and Carolyn resists the urge to throw her wallet at the wall in lieu of swatting him. "I'm serious, Caro, you've been running around nonstop for the past week."

"I know." Carolyn rests her head on the back of the couch. She doesn't tell Alex it's because she's trying to forget the words her mother wrote about her, but she also hasn't forgotten about what Josh said to her outside the funeral home. She wants Josh to be right and her mother to be wrong. She wants to pretend that her mother's words didn't make her worry that they were true. She wants to tell her mother the truth she didn't get to, that she's going to reach the future she planned for herself, but it's taking her more time than she thought because of how getting into med school works. She wants to tell Mom that she will be successful, that she can push the Hawkins name ever closer to the glass ceiling.

Carolyn knows she won't get that chance, and she hates that she'll never be able to put right that miscommunication. She hates that she'll carry this smoldering pit in her stomach for the rest of her life, that the shadow of doubt will always be cast over her head and squeeze around her heart.

But she will have to live with it, somehow.

Carolyn sits up and calls to Alex in the kitchen, "Are you making something?"

"If by 'making something' you mean heating up one of the seventeen dishes people have brought for us in the past week, then sure, I'm making something." Alex emerges from the kitchen balancing three dishes of Lori's broccoli casserole on his arms.

"Those days of waiting tables pay off." Josh gets up from the couch to grab one of the dishes.

"Honestly, comes in handy," Alex says, sitting down in Mom's usual armchair next to the TV and poking his fork into the dish. "Caro, I know you hate this question, but how are you doing?"

Carolyn puffs a sigh and shifts on the couch. "I'm doing okay, I guess." But the purple notebook pokes her in the thigh, and suddenly she has to get rid of it. She sets her casserole down and pulls it out of her pocket.

Alex's eyes widen as she tosses it on the table. "Caro, I didn't know you had that at the funeral."

Carolyn shifts back and picks up her casserole again. Avoids meeting her brother's eyes.

She could give Alex the real answer to his implied question. She could tell him about her mother's words, her fear that Skylar Garnet was right about her the way mothers always are, her worry that she won't be able to prove to her mother that she can in fact make her proud without needing an extra push. She could tell him that now all she wants is to put right the misunderstanding Mom has about her, the one she carried with her to the very end. She could tell him she wants their mother to see her sparkle and that bringing the journal to the funeral today was, in a way, the first step toward proving to her mother what she could become.

But Carolyn also remembers countless late-night conversations with her mother about boys and girls, careers, schools and other miscellaneous stresses. She remembers Mom teaching her to change a tire when she was fifteen and also showing her the best way to hold a makeup brush. The security in going to bed and hearing the TV turned on low downstairs, knowing her mother was playing something in the background as she worked. Carolyn knows her mother would have moved the moon for her if she'd asked her to.

When Carolyn glances at Josh, he lifts his shoulders in a slight shrug as if to say, *Up to you.*

Carolyn scoops a forkful of broccoli casserole and meets Alex's gaze. "I guess I just wanted a piece of her with me today."

Which, she realizes, is also true.

# 3.
# TO FOLLOW A STAR

*Pippa, 23, Rockingworth Point (WA, USA), 2019*
*"How did I not see that you wanted to let go?"*

My fingers tap a rhythm on the panel by the driver's side window, my hand brushing against the fogged-up glass as the familiar soft gray-and-blue-sided houses of Rockingworth Point roll by. "My Calling" by AJR blasts from my speakers, the bass turned up high. When I reach the dented mailbox two houses away from Aunt Mara's house, I turn the volume down.

I kill the ignition and let my Mini Cooper sit in the driveway. Watch the front door. Wait for Aunt Mara to swing it open in dark jeans and her favorite burnt-orange sweater, black hair pulled into a topknot on her head. Wait for that eager wave as I get out of the car, for the sweet smell of her floral and citrus perfume drifting after her as she goes to engulf me in a tight hug. Wait for her to usher me into the kitchen, where she has lemon bars or molasses cookies or cinnamon meringues sitting out on the counter for us as she talks a mile a minute about the new recipe she's tried this week in between asking me how my week is going.

I know she's not coming, of course, but I wait anyway, hoping. Just for a little. Wanting her back, so I can do just one thing differently.

I get out of the car, head up the set stone path alone, turn the key in the front door, and push it open, listening to the hinges creak and the sharp October breeze as it sweeps in, rustling the mail in the basket next to the door. I've been here alone plenty of times for our regular weekend visits but never when Aunt Mara wasn't home and not since she died four months ago.

    Even so, I'm only here right now because Aunt Mara told me and Ma, four and a half months ago in the note she left, that she'd taken care of everything except the attic, and that she wanted me to go up there and finish that off. There wasn't much of my stuff left up there, because the older I'd gotten, the fewer of my actual belongings stayed here. The constants were the bean bag she'd gotten for me when I was born and the photo frames, although their contents changed as we both got older. Ma offered to come today, but I wanted to do it alone. The attic was our space – just me and Aunt Mara.

    Maybe, if I'd said something, it could still be our space.

    I climb the front stairs and stop at the base of the ladder, looking at the entrance overhead. Two sets of footsteps echo as I climb the ladder without really touching the sides and poke my head into the attic. It's bigger than I remember, although it's barely been four months since I was last here after graduation and nothing has changed. The photo frames still stand on the shelves; the throw I keep on the beanbag is still folded but slightly askew. My own face looks back at me, the only thing visible in the full-length mirror from this angle. Black hair past my shoulders, almond-shaped brown eyes with a touch of mascara on the lashes. My expression is neutral, my face the same as it was four months ago. Nothing in this attic has changed, yet everything has changed, my reality reshaped around me. The burden of oblivion, for instance, that will rest on my shoulders for the rest of time.

I set my purse on the beanbag and pull my hair into a topknot. If I want to be done and back home before dark, I have about two hours to decide what's happening to everything in the attic, pack it up, and haul it down to my car to start the five-hour drive home. I could stay here tonight, I suppose, but I'd be alone.

I start my workout playlist on my phone so there's something alive in this house besides me and get to work to "100 Bad Days" by AJR. One of the boxes in the corner is empty; it used to hold my stuffed animals, but as I've gotten older, most of them have been donated to the pediatric ward at the hospital, except my Winnie the Pooh and my Piglet who stay on my bed at home, safe and in good company. Aunt Mara was good about making sure that we kept paring down as I got older.

In hindsight, I wonder if it might have been part of a larger plan.

I move fast, pulling photo frames down from the shelf, the few books I still keep here—*The From-Aways*, *Half of a Yellow Sun*, *Golden*. At the bottom of the shelf, I stop and crouch down. This is new.

One of those yellow-orange envelopes – the kind Ma always uses to send documents to our family living overseas—sits on the bottom shelf. It has my name on it in Aunt Mara's handwriting—a distinctive, looping, cursive scrawl that slants to the right. It covers pages of recipe books I've grown up with, birthday cards, and Christmas cards. She always signs them the same way: *Love, Aunt Mara. P.S.: I'm so proud of you. You're going to do great things!*

I take the envelope from the shelf, sit down on the carpet, and flip it over. It's heavy, even for one of these big things. For a minute, I consider taking it down to the kitchen—I know where the scissors are—but I like being ensconced in the attic. It's our space, after all.

I reach for the phone and turn the music down so that AJR's "Karma" stops echoing through the house. I tear the envelope open, wincing when it rips down instead of across. *Sorry, Aunt Mara.*

A thick wad of paper emerges. Loose sheets and envelopes scatter everywhere, and I scrabble to pull them back into a pile. When I flip the papers over, my aunt's handwriting jumps out at me, and there's a card on top.

> *Dearest Pippa,*
>
> *There aren't enough words to express quite how proud I am. I am so grateful for the years we have had together, the years during which I was able to watch you grow, your aspirations develop, your heart open. What it is you're going to do, exactly, I don't know, but I know they're going to be great things. I hope that from wherever I am, I will be able to see you go on to follow your dreams, to accomplish all those things you've said you wanted to do. End world poverty. Become a polyglot. Study the ocean and protect it and the creatures who live in it. Hell, go and judge figure-skating if you want to, even though we've both never really skated. God knows we've watched enough to understand way more than the average spectator. The day we had the revelation that the difference between a triple toe loop and a triple lutz is all in which leg the skater lands on was a good day.*
>
> *I wanted to make sure that your graduation gift would be something you could keep on you, though you may not receive this until after. I wanted to make sure it was*

*something you could treasure through life. I hope I've done well here.*
    *Congratulations, sweetie. And remember, always try to catch the stars.*

*Love always,*
*Aunt Mara*

I chew on my lower lip. That last sentence drifts around my mind, echoes through the attic from various voices over the years. "*Catch the stars, Pippa. You'll see what can happen.*"

*****

A soft knock on the door jolts me out of sleep, and I stay in bed, warm and drowsy and the blankets heavy over me, even in midsummer. My voice is hazy when I mumble, "Hello?"

The hallway behind her is dark, so I can only see her shadow as Aunt Mara whispers, "Good, you're awake. Come with me, I want to show you something."

I sit up in bed, alert now. "What is it?"

"You'll see."

My seven-year-old curiosity piqued, I slide out from between my covers and pad over to Aunt Mara, waiting at my bedroom door. It's not my bedroom door, really, because this is Aunt Mara's house and not mine, but Aunt Mara always tells me it's my own special room when I come here to stay with her and Uncle Xin. When I look up at her, I see her eyes gleaming, starry with excitement, and I'm excited, too, though I don't know why.

"Come on." Aunt Mara takes my hand and guides me toward the attic ladder.

"Where's Uncle Xin?" I whisper, clutching Aunt Mara's hand tightly.

"He's sleeping." Aunt Mara stops at the bottom of the ladder. "Are you ready?"

"What are we doing?" Now that my eyes have adjusted to the dark, I can see my aunt's face more clearly, bright and eager, like my best friend Ashleigh when she gets excited about our volleyball unit in P.E. class.

"It's a surprise."

I look up at the ladder, ascending toward a yawning hole in the ceiling. What if it swallows me whole? What if my stuffed animals are up there, leading secret midnight lives they don't want me to see?

"Come. I'll go up first, okay?" Aunt Mara takes the ladder, and it creaks softly beneath her weight as she climbs up, her feet nearly soundless. I wait until she's halfway up before following, scrambling to keep up with her so that whatever might be behind me can't catch me.

When my head pokes up into the attic, Aunt Mara is already waiting at the window facing the yard and the beach. She's propped it open, too. My arms tingle as I shake them out and the blood rushes back into them. A soft breeze drifts in, playing across my face and tugging at my hair, and I shiver and bring my feet up into the attic. I can't help shooting a furtive look around, half-hoping that I might see my stuffed animals sitting in a circle to talk the way we do at school, but they're asleep under their blankets where I left them.

"Come on, Pip." Aunt Mara pushes up the window screen. "I want to show you something."

"Where are we going?"

"The roof."

"Are we allowed to?"

"Of course."

I shiver, but I pad over to her anyway, my feet soundless on the blue rug Aunt Mara laid down when we first set up the attic together. "Are you sure?"

"Of course. Come on." Aunt Mara smiles, and I'm instantly warmer. "Are you cold? Here."

She holds out a blanket, but she's just far enough away from the window that I have to climb out of it to get to her. So I do, squeezing my body through the tiny space and only bumping my knee on the sill as I pull my left foot out.

"Good job." Aunt Mara smiles. "Close the screen, sweetie."

Once it's shut, she waves me over. The shingles of the roof lightly prickle the bottoms of my feet, but Aunt Mara has laid out another blanket, and she hands me the blanket she's been holding and sits down when I reach her. "Come sit."

I wrap the blanket around my shoulders like a cape and sit down, hugging my knees to my chest so that the blanket can cover everything. "What's the surprise?"

Aunt Mara leans back to rest on her elbows and points to the sky. "Look."

I want to copy her, but I'm too cold. Instead, I tilt my head back. Above me, the stars swirl together, a brilliant silver tapestry against a dark velvet sky, and my head tips to one side as I lean back all the way and adjust the blanket to keep me covered. I've visited Aunt Mara here many times, with and without Ma and Dad, but I've never gone out on to the roof, never seen the stars spread out before me like this.

I love that Aunt Mara's house is by the beach, that it's only five hours away. It means we can basically go whenever Ma or Dad decide they want to. It means I can stand on the beach and watch the ocean forever. It's restless, always tossing and turning over, like me when I can't fall asleep at night. When it's warm out, I can curl my toes in the warm sand, feel its softness before running down to meet the waves as they land on the beach, their gentle murmur from afar an inviting call.

On summer nights, we sit around our fire pit in the yard and roast marshmallows for s'mores. Uncle Xin cracks a joke about how he's going to have to keep building the fire higher if he wants it to stay the same size as me. Aunt Mara takes my arm and points to the stars, and I always follow her finger, but I usually can't see more than a few. The fire snaps and pops, and it's so bright, dancing orange and yellow, that I'm always pulled back to earth.

"You see that?" Aunt Mara says now, pointing up at the stars and tracing the shape of a spoon with her finger. "That's the Big Dipper. And over there"—her finger moves slightly up and over, tracing a new shape—"that's the Little Dipper."

I try hard to see the shapes she's pointing out, but I can't make anything out. It all looks like one big silver carpet to me, but I nod anyway. I know it doesn't matter too much to her, whether I know the shapes the stars make in the sky.

"Do you know what the stars are called all together?"

I have to think hard. We talked about this in science during the week. My teacher likened it to a candy bar. "The Milky Way?"

"Good job. High-five." Aunt Mara holds a hand up, and I give her the high-five, pleased with myself for remembering.

"Do you think we can go to the stars?"

"Not right now. But maybe one day. You'll figure out how to get to them."

"Are you sure we can't go right now?"

Aunt Mara laughs softly. "I don't think so. But I'll tell you something." She sits up and gestures at the stars, spreads her arms wide. "All those stars? You know what they look like?"

I turn to look at her, her face serene, years of wisdom and mystery behind her eyes that I wanted so badly to know. "What do they look like?"

"They look like dreams." Aunt Mara turns to me and smiles.

I squint up at the sky. I only see stars, close together and far apart, dotting the black sky. Some of them wink at me, friendly. I am suddenly warmer, and the stars are suddenly closer, but I still don't understand. "How do they look like dreams?"

Aunt Mara's voice is dreamy as she replies, "You'll see when you try to catch them."

\*\*\*

There are seven sealed envelopes and twenty-three loose sheets of paper. Aunt Mara's distinctive scrawl loops across every sheet, lines dancing and swirling across the paper in a way that only she can create. As I flip through the sheets, I catch the dates, always in the top right-hand corner. Most of them are January 1, the beginning of every year since I was born. On the last loose letter, the most recent one, I recognize the date of my college graduation, a few months ago now. My lips twist to one side.

I shuffle through the envelopes, painstakingly labeled. *For hard times. For good times. For the night of your wedding – if you so choose. For breakups. For when you need a boost. For when you miss me.*

When my eyes land on the last one, I bite my lip. This envelope is thicker than the others.

My phone buzzes on the table, and I glance at the screen. A text from Ma. *All okay?*

*Yeah. Just found some stuff I didn't know was here. I'll still be home by tonight though.* I hit 'Send' before I start thinking too much about the wording of the second sentence.

My phone buzzes again. Ma, sending a thumbs-up emoji.

I chew on my lower lip. I should talk to Ma more about Aunt Mara, but our lives after her death have gone on as usual. She went back to work a week after the funeral, mostly since Aunt Mara made sure to get everything sorted before she died, and there wasn't much left for us to do. She'd taken care of all of it months before, we discovered. The house, her savings, the photo albums to Ma. The books to me. Her clothes for the two of us "to fight over," as she said in her will, which was really a more formalized version of her note. And we did fight over them, in the middle of July, trading jokes about which shirt I got to keep and whether this one pair of jeans Ma had always secretly wanted would actually fit her.

That last one didn't quite sit right with me. Actually, none of this sat right with me, maybe because I wish I'd seen that something wasn't sitting right with Aunt Mara. Or that Ma had seen something. But I remember the color draining from Ma's face the day we got the call. She had no idea. No inkling that her sister had arranged her death and its circumstances months before, behind closed doors, while we blindly celebrated my college graduation the week before and blew past how much Aunt Mara was hurting, how much she had been hurting for years.

***

I tap my feet on the back porch of Aunt Mara's house, sliding them back and forth over the boards. I count the number of lines that slip beneath the tips of my flip-flops. I've been sitting out here for twenty minutes in one of the two curved wicker armchairs wrapped in a blanket and trying to read, but my ears are straining to catch words from inside, and I haven't turned a page in fifteen minutes. In the yard next to Aunt Mara's, I watch the neighbor let his dog out, watch the tiny terrier whip around excitedly, its tail up like a flag.

The back door creaks, and my head whips around. I want it to be Aunt Mara because I've hardly seen her this weekend, but it's only Ma. Her black hair is up in a knot behind her head, held together with a massive jaw clip. The shadows under her eyes are like bruises. Pronounced, like they have been for the past three weeks. Aunt Mara has been staying at our house for the past two. My sixteenth birthday celebration with my family, two days after she arrived, was a subdued affair. We're only at Aunt Mara's this weekend to pick up some fresh clothes and check on the house plants.

I offer my arms for a hug anyway, and she wraps her arms around my shoulders and drops a kiss on my head. "Where's Aunt Mara?" I ask.

"She's taking a nap." Ma sits down in the other curved wicker chair next to me, her eyes glazing over as they fasten idly on the little terrier running around in the other yard. "I guess the divorce is harder for her than she thought it would be."

"Why does it have to be so hard? Uncle Xin cheated on her, so she's better off without him, right?"

"Honey, it's a lot more complicated than that." Ma turns her eyes away from the sea and meets my gaze. "She really loved him, you know? And they were together for a really long time, since before college. It's hard for something that lasted for twenty years to just… end."

"I guess." I look away, back at the terrier, who is sniffing intently at the holly bushes at the end of their yard. I'm mad because I liked Uncle Xin, because he bought me so many of the books that live in the attic at their house that I read and reread every time I'm here. Because he was the first one to offer me wine at Christmas dinner last year, with a sneaky wink and a raised eyebrow. It was bitter, sour almost, but I felt like an adult for a second, holding the wine glass by its stem. Because all of these bright snippets of memory I have are now tainted, distorted by Aunt Mara's tears and the unfamiliar smell of coconut water that lingered on Uncle Xin's clothes. "Did she know?"

I can feel Ma looking at me as she says, "She suspected. But she didn't know for sure until she came home early from a work trip, and there they were, in their own house."

"That... sucks." I don't know what else to say, but I glance over my shoulder, into the house where Aunt Mara had caught them. Where Aunt Mara and Uncle Xin had, instantly, become two completely different people.

"Yeah." Ma puffs a sigh, tilts her head back, and closes her eyes. "Don't worry about her, honey. She'll pick up eventually; she knows how to." On the other side of the house, on the street, a car honks. "Let me know if she seems off to you, though, okay? I want to make sure she's sorted before I let her go stay in this big house alone, but I'd rather not bring it up if she doesn't want to talk about it."

"I will." Ma and Aunt Mara talk, I know they do, but Aunt Mara talks differently to Ma than she does to me. With Ma and Aunt Mara, it's memories of their college days and people they used to know. With Aunt Mara and me, it's figure skating when the competitions are on or performances we missed, thoughts ranging from whether a bee could take a wasp in a fight to how soon we're all going to succumb to climate change, and new recipes. Ma and I mostly talk about school and work and their respective dramas, up until recently, with Aunt Mara and Uncle Xin's relationship on the rocks.

Now, something occurs to me, and I turn to Ma. "Maybe she'll find someone else."

Ma smiles slightly. "Maybe she will."

For a while, the sea rolls up and down the beach, murmuring softly in our ears, and then Ma asks, "Did Ashleigh ever sort out that fight between those two girls on the volleyball team?"

"Oh, boy," I say, thinking of the week Ashleigh had had trying to keep the girls' varsity team together during our high school league tournament even though Christine Xiao and Darcy Lehman weren't speaking to each other because of a test grade—I didn't know the details. "I don't know if she sorted it out, but they made it through."

"So, what happened?" Ma asks, and I turn a little so that I'm facing her, wrap the blanket a little closer around my shoulders as a breeze sweeps through the screened porch, and I launch into my tale.

\*\*\*

I reach for the envelope labeled *For hard times*, spin it around between my palms, hold it out in front of me, then flip it around to open it. Inside, a single folded sheet of paper.

*Dearest Pippa,*
*Hard times are inevitable. It's a fact of life. And they're always painful. But it's how nature works. Like the tides,*

*always changing; like the waves, moving up and down the beach. Sometimes they crash down, and you're blindsided. Sometimes you know they're coming. Either way, it doesn't make it easier. What matters is what you do in the aftermath, when the water washes back and you're left there on the beach. Which has happened to you. I've watched you get knocked over by the waves countless times, even when you were fifteen and you were so embarrassed about it that you wouldn't let me tell your ma.*

*I know you don't like clichés, so I'm not going to fill you with those. What I will say is that some of them are true, for some of us. Time does help. It does heal wounds. And in that time, you have to figure out how to deal with the things that are hard. There's no one way to do it, as long as it helps you.*

*The only thing I ask is that you always, always pick yourself up. Like Madison Chock and Evan Bates when they fell during their dance at the 2018 Olympics. They got up and they finished their dance with grace, and they didn't let that one mistake define their Olympic experience. Move past it. And keep reaching for what you want.*

*I didn't say that doing this would be easy. You'll be wobbling at first, balancing on thin blades on a thinner sheet of ice. I only ask you to do it, no matter how hard it gets, because I know that you can.*

*I'll know if you haven't done it.*

*Love always,*<br>*Aunt Mara*

I almost laugh. Oh, the irony. *Always, always pick yourself up.* But I can't be mad at her because she tried, for six long years, to pick herself up. She tried so hard, in fact, that none of us knew she couldn't do it. None of us knew how much she hated herself for still loving him, day after week after month after year. Not Ma, not Dad, not me.

Shouldn't we have noticed?

I want to be mad at her for hiding it from us. From me. But I know who I'm really angry with. And it's not Aunt Mara.

\*\*\*

"What do you think happens when you die?" Aunt Mara asks. We're sitting on the roof of her house together, and I'm twenty-one now and really can't fit out the window anymore, but we make a point of squeezing out here at least once every time I come.

I raise my eyebrows. "Where did that come from?"

"Oh, I don't know." Aunt Mara smiles. I'm surprised by the question, because it's come out of the blue, but I'm always glad when she talks to me like this, because it reminds me that I'm a friend just as much as I am her niece. "Don't you just wonder that sometimes?"

"Yeah. You know, the weirdest thing is that Ashleigh and I were having that conversation just the other day." It's true. We were. She's reading *Slaughterhouse Five* again as part of her work for her thesis, and whenever she reads it, she gets existential.

"What did Ashleigh say?"

"That whatever you believe in is where you go." I pull my knees into my chest, mimicking her. When I look at my aunt, her gaze is on the sea and the beach, and her eyes are glazing over, with that faraway look she gets whenever we talk about the stars. "What do you think?"

"I don't know what happens after death." Aunt Mara's voice is dreamy. The sea is calm today, a gentle murmur with the occasional loud sigh. The tide is receding. "But I guess we all find out eventually, don't we?"

"Yeah, we do." I keep watching her, but her gaze remains steadfast, fastened on the waves that crest and tumble in the distance.

"Do you think it's something good?" Aunt Mara asks.

I tilt my head. Think about what Ma said when I asked her the same question—that people go wherever their actions will lead them. "I think it depends on the person and what they believe in."

Aunt Mara nods, a slow movement of her head tipping back and forth. Her body follows, rocking, back, forth, back, forth, as though following the waves that sing up and down the sand. "I hope it's something good."

\*\*\*

*For when you miss me.* I want to open it, but the envelope is so much thicker than the others. What is she going to tell me?

Will I want to hear it?

My phone buzzes on the ground. Another text from Ma. *Look what I found.* It's a picture of a picture from one of Aunt Mara's many photo albums, of her and Ma together from their college days. It always gives me a jolt to see them together, twenty years younger, looking so much like their older selves with so much less weight on their shoulders. They are sitting in the pizza parlor that always figures in their college reminiscences, with huge slices in front of them on paper plates. Aunt Mara is wearing a Santa hat, for some reason. She is laughing at the camera, her whole face is, dark eyes lit up against her light skin. Ma, too, is laughing, pointing at whoever's taking the picture, her black hair loose and so much longer than it is now.

My fingers hover over the tiny touch keyboard, then bang out a response. *Omg. Can we look at those when I get home?*

Ma's reply is immediate. *Of course!*

I really should ask her if she ever felt something was off in the five years after Aunt Mara and Uncle Xin officially got their divorce settled. If Aunt Mara ever said anything to her that she wishes she'd thought more about. If she feels as guilty as I do for not noticing anything in the six years since Aunt Mara had first found out that Uncle Xin was cheating on her. But our family—we don't talk about these things. Easier to talk about who could beat Wonder Woman in a fight than about what we want after death. For all the random thoughts that occurred to Aunt Mara and me—those really personal ones—my parents and I always skirted around them.

Maybe we shouldn't have.

For a moment, I stare at my phone screen and the text that floats at my fingertips, just waiting to hit 'Send.' *Can we talk about everything?* But instead, I hit delete, hold the key down until the words disappear. Ma loves to talk about Aunt Mara but not about the end.

I flip over the envelope that says *For when you miss me.* There's a tiny post-script in the bottom right-hand corner. *Please show this one to your mother.*

I chew on my lower lip and text Ma. *Found something Aunt Mara wanted me to show you. Can look at it when I get back too.*

I don't wait for her response. Instead, I shove my phone in my back pocket and the envelope back in the yellow one. I collect all the papers, stack them neatly, and finish packing up what's left. There are still some books left that Uncle Xin gave me, and I can't bring myself to get rid of them because some of them are my favorites, despite the six years of silence that have gone by between us and everything he did that hurt Aunt Mara.

Thirty-seven minutes later, the box is in the backseat of my Mini Cooper and the rug is rolled up on the floor. The beanbag chair is stuffed in the seat next to the box, and I know I'm done, but I'm still standing in the attic clutching Aunt Mara's yellow envelope to my chest, looking around for something I might have forgotten.

Something I might have missed.

I cross the attic, letting my fingers drift along the worn wood of the windowsill. There's a dent in the right-hand corner from where Aunt Mara's shoe kicked it a little too hard; there's a long scratch on the left side where I dragged one of my heels against it when I crawled out the window so Aunt Mara could take my high school senior pictures, well over four years ago now. Aunt Mara's petite, so she's always been able to fit out the window, but the window has been too small for me to fit through easily since I started high school.

I open the window and lift the sash and screen and try to wriggle my body through the thing anyway, cursing when I nearly overbalance because I'm clutching the envelope to my chest with one arm and only have one free arm to help me balance. My hips get stuck and I have to contort my body around, banging one knee into the shingles of the roof when my hips finally pop free. That will bruise tomorrow for sure.

I step over to the edge of the roof, pull my hair out of my topknot and stick it in a ponytail, and gaze out on the back view. It's midday, the sun sparkling high over the sea. The beach is quiet—it's mid-October, after all—but even from up here, through the sharp wind, I can hear the waves lapping on the sand, watch the water swell, crest, tumble, recede.

I'm waiting for Aunt Mara to say something, I realize. To tell me what to do.

The breeze plays across my face, soft, tangling tiny baby hairs. I hold out Aunt Mara's thick envelope, dangling it over the edge of the roof. There's only sand and a stone path leading to the beach behind the house, but in the distance, I can see the waves, cresting and falling. The breeze is sharp. The envelope sways, thick with the weight of paper and last words. The ground's a long way away.

The envelope twists in the air, dropping to the ground. Almost taken by the wind if not for its weight, and lands with a soft thud in the sand below that sends tiny grains scattering.

How easy was it to let go?

Something swoops and clenches in my stomach. In an instant, I'm wrestling my way back through the window, scrambling down the attic ladder, and thundering down the front stairs with my black ponytail flying over my shoulder. My feet skid slightly on the tiles as I run through the kitchen and throw open the screen door to the back porch. The envelope is still there, its yellow artificial and almost orange color against the sand.

I snatch it up. Brush it off. It's still in pristine condition, but there's a dent in the sand where it landed. A sigh shudders through me as I smooth my hand over the indentations the black pen has made in the envelope. Overhead, a cloud glides over the sun, shielding me from its full brightness even as it glitters off the water in the distance, and I remember Aunt Mara with me, age seven, on the roof, reminding me that the sun is also a star. As the cloud turns, one of its rays peeks out, blinking at me, friendly, as though it is extending a hand.

I turn away, eyes stinging, and pull out the last envelope. *For when you miss me.*

I slide my finger under the flap, needing first to see it for myself.

# 4.

# PINEAPPLES

*Dean, 22, Boston (MA, USA), 2015*
*"What if doing one thing differently could have changed everything?"*

"Dean, hey, you're not joining us for lunch today?"

I pull my Tupperware with my fajitas out of the microwave and offer Shana a tight smile. "No, I've got to take care of a few things today. I'll see you guys after."

I don't wait for their responses as I stride out of the break room. Too bad if I seem rude. I can make amends later. I know Shana means well, and I usually like hanging out with everyone in the office at lunch. It's a great crew. They're funny, and they always make that extra effort to include me. I usually sit with them, because I'm just an intern and I have to build those connections however I can, but I really need to be alone today.

I can't try to handle the anniversary of Ben's death around strangers who didn't know him.

I take my Tupperware down the stairs and out the front doors into the warm midsummer Boston humidity. The second I'm out the office doors, I can feel some of the tension leaving my shoulders, and I cross the street to get down to the Charles River Esplanade so I can catch a bit of a breeze and some peace and quiet.

My Tupperware shakes a little in my hands as I cross the path and find a tree on the long stretch of grass a little farther away from people picnicking in the shade out of the summer heat. Sticks litter the ground around me as I sit down, finally alone.

Well, not exactly. I came down here for a reason.

***

"Hey, Ben. Can you hear me?

"I don't know if you can hear me. But I'm going to talk to you anyways, and I'm going to imagine you're here in Boston, sitting in front of me in khakis and one of your Vanderbilt sweatshirts from your endless supply, because having you in front of me makes this feel a little less like I'm a crazy guy talking under a tree and more like I'm really talking to you.

"Okay, I won't lie, I feel kind of awkward. I know I've got my headphones in to make it look like I'm just on the phone with you, but I still feel like someone's going to walk by this tree and realize what's really happening. Because obviously, I'm not actually on the phone with you. And then I'm going to have to explain everything, and I'd really rather not do that. Honestly, I really don't want to talk to anyone about you except you. I don't talk much about you unless it's with my buddies and someone mentions something that reminds me of you.

"Jakub's been texting me asking if I'm okay, and I've been telling him yeah, I'm fine, but there's still a lot to think about today. And I know he likes hearing about you, and I like it when he listens, because he doesn't care if I lose my shit and start crying or punching something for God knows what reason. He just lets me get it out of my system when it gets really bad and doesn't care what comes out of my mouth. And, like, I know he's my best friend at Boston, but I just feel like today is about you, you know? Not about me and how I'm feeling. Which is sort of stupid, I guess, because the ones who feel you the most are the ones who got left behind, and we all share that, so it's supposed to be fine. Like, I know it is, intellectually, but it just feels wrong, you know?

"God, I can hear you now. 'Dean, calm down. These kinds of anniversaries are always hard, so if you want to talk, it's fine. And watch your shoes. If you ruin those Air Force Ones I got you, I'll kill you. Those were a birthday gift, you better take care of them.'

"Just so you know, I've been taking care of them. But I don't actually wear them much. I only do when I want to have you with me on whatever day it is. We're not technically supposed to wear sneakers to the office, but these are bright white and if you weren't paying attention, you wouldn't really notice. Anyway, they look nice enough that no one's said anything about it so far.

"It's been a year, you know. Well, of course, you know that. I haven't been counting every day because who needs to, really? Everyone knows there's 365 days in a year, so we don't need to count them to remind us that time is passing but somehow bringing us back to where we started.

"But I have been counting down the days in recent weeks. Dreading today. The only anniversaries I've had are ones that are different from yours—relationships, graduations, Facebook friends. What the fuck is a death anniversary supposed to be like? What am I supposed to do? I feel like I'm supposed to be doing something else to remember you, something besides sitting here under this tree and talking out loud to myself, to you. Like, maybe I should have driven to Vandy today or something. But that would probably have taken twice as long since I'm in Boston and not home in DC.

"I still want to know why, you know? I think about that a lot. There are so many fatal car accidents, but I keep thinking about how ridiculous it is, all the little factors that put you in the position to get your car rear-ended by that particular truck. All I know is that you left my apartment early because you wanted to avoid rush-hour traffic getting out of DC, and I went right back to bed after you left because it was really early and honestly, I was only half-awake when I said bye to you. And I don't know anything else in between, so now all I can think about are the what-ifs. What if you never saw the truck coming? What if you saw the truck and you changed lanes to avoid it, but it hit you anyway?

"What if all of this could have been avoided by changing one thing?

"Look, I know you'd tell me to shut up with all these questions. Like, I can hear you saying that nothing can be changed, and what's done is over and done with, so I should stop thinking about it. I can't change it. And you're right, but it's harder to accept that when the thing that's over and done with is your life.

"It was mid-morning, too. Just after rush hour. And you were going the other way from all that traffic. It was just that damn merge by Nutley that always gets bottlenecked because once people get on the highway, they forget how to drive.

"The truck was carrying pineapples. Isn't that ridiculous? Just a truck driving down the freeway, carrying pineapples to God knows where. The image of the pineapples spilling out of the back of the truck, bouncing and rolling around the asphalt—that's so funny to me. I know you would have laughed—not about the near-misses that all of those rolling pineapples caused, but about the absurdity of hundreds and hundreds of pineapples rolling around on the freeway, diving and swerving under the wheels of cars and trucks."

\*\*\*

My phone buzzes in my lap, and I blink, my eyes darting from the lazy flow of the river to the bright screen. Dad. *All okay?*

I grit my teeth, shut my eyes. I'm not mad at him for checking in. He's like Shana—he means well—but the difference is, he knows that on this day last year, my best friend since kindergarten died.

I bang out a short response. *Yes.* I shouldn't be so annoyed, but my flow's been interrupted now. I'd just been starting to feel less awkward.

Once my text to Dad is gone, I turn off all notifications and lean my head back against the tree.

\*\*\*

"Sorry. Dad texted me. Can't leave him hanging. I can't seem to do that to anyone anymore.

"Where was I? Oh, right, the pineapples on the road. You know, I bet the news would be on that right away, and they'd probably publish it before they knew all the facts about where those pineapples came from. They're always on the sensational. I'm pretty sure you were the one who told me that, actually. You always hated those clickbait headlines, because they worked, and you hated that they worked.

"You'd get that headline on your phone, probably, and you'd text it to me if we were at school or show it to me across the table if we were hanging out. I'd probably laugh, out loud, and then feel stupid for laughing because no one else would get the joke. Say something like, 'Man, I hope those pineapples didn't cause too many accidents.'

"If we were together, you would probably laugh too, sit back from your phone where this headline would have just come up on Apple News or some shit. You'd probably run a hand through your hair even though you never need to fix that brown flow. And then you'd give me that crooked grin that always looks smugger than it's supposed to be. 'I mean, I hope so too, but that's fucking hilarious. Can you imagine, just, like, pineapples rolling all over the road?' And I'd really picture it, and then I'd laugh even though I wouldn't want to be laughing, because car accidents aren't funny.

"Your car was totaled. It was so bad. I bet you're pissed about that. When your dad called, he couldn't really speak, but he said the car was totally mangled, front end and driver door completely crushed and everything. He said you were gone. And I was so calm, it was kind of weird. Honestly, I barely remember that day, but I remember feeling my face go completely cold, and I just sat there on my bed, kind of numb. Same feeling I got when I stood up to talk about you at the funeral. I felt like you were supposed to be sitting in the front row next to your parents, giving me that smug grin and a thumbs-up because you know I hate public speaking.

"But I had to do it, man. I felt like if I didn't say something, it would be like I was agreeing to forget about you, so I stood up there in front of everyone and talked about high school and our annual visits and all those hours we spent just sitting in your car talking about stuff that was important, like where we wanted to go to college, or stuff that made no sense. Like pineapples, I guess.

"Man, you really loved that car. I mean, I don't need to tell you this, because you already know it, but I think about that sometimes, you know? You got it as an eighteenth birthday present, right before senior year. It drove you and me from your house to school every day after you got it. Remember when we'd fight about the aux cord until you finally said, 'Fuck it, let's have a rotating system,' and then we took turns blasting EDM and hip-hop every morning? And then half the time when you'd drop me off somewhere or we were going somewhere together, we wouldn't get out of the car for another twenty minutes because we'd be mid-conversation or something when we got to wherever we were going. So we'd keep talking, and at least one of us would end up being late.

"And then, when we started college, it took you from DC to Vanderbilt every year, you and all your shit for move-in day that you hadn't put in storage. Even though it's an Audi Q5 and it's a decent size, I really never understood how you managed to fit everything into one car. I was terrible at it. Still am. You laughed at me once, for my shitty packing job. But I guess you use storage, so that wasn't fair. Plus, you're good at packing."

\*\*\*

My head tips forward from against the tree trunk, and I frown. I've caught myself doing it again. Talking about Ben like he's still here. Even a year later, I still do that sometimes. And it's weird because I know he's gone, but sometimes, it's almost like I forget that.

Across the river, two guys are throwing a Frisbee back and forth, and their shouts just barely drift to me even though I can't catch what they're saying. For a moment, I am back in DC beside the Potomac, and it is four years earlier. I'm laughing my ass off as Ben tries to fish a Frisbee out from the muddy water, leaning as far out as he can over the surface to try and reach it without getting wet. But we both know it's long gone.

I blink the memory from behind my eyes as a stick pokes me in the leg.

\*\*\*

"Sorry. Got distracted again. Sometimes those memories really just come out of nowhere. Especially today. Some days, everything reminds me of you.

"The other day, Post Malone came on the radio, and I went back to freshman year, when you drove all the way from Vandy to Boston to visit me at school. And I just remembered when you rolled up outside my dorm you had the bass cranked all the way up and the windows all the way down and Post Malone just blasting out the windows. You even opened the sunroof, in the middle of a Boston winter. All my buddies were so hyped. Jakub told me later he'd have to tell his friends that if they came to visit, that's the entrance they'd have to beat. That's what my Boston friends think of you. You're cool-entrance-guy to them, basically. I mean, not only that, because we all hung out together for a weekend, but whenever I mention your name, they're like 'Oh, yeah, he was the one who rolled up blasting Post Malone that one time, right? He was awesome.'

"I bet you like that legacy.

"You know, I don t really know where I'm going with this. I guess it's just crazy to think about, you know? Like, that truck took out you and your car. Both gone because of one crash. And you were just trying to get home on time from visiting me so you could get enough sleep and still make it to work the next day. You're such a safe driver, too. Like, you never texted and drove at the same time. You'd barely pick up the phone even when it was connected to the Bluetooth in your car, and when you did, the conversations were always a couple of minutes, max. 'I'm driving,' you'd say, 'but I'll text you when I'm back so I can talk to you properly.'

"Why'd I go back to bed? Fuck.

"I can hear your voice right now—'Dean, that's a stupid question. It's not like you'd have stopped it if you'd been awake. I was miles away by that point.'

"And, like—yeah, I know that. But do you know how fucking awful it was to wake up to the phone ringing and see that it was your dad? The only other time your dad called me was when you went to the hospital for appendicitis. You were so high off the painkillers and you kept asking him to call me and tell me that I didn't have to worry. I didn't even know there was something I was supposed to be worried about until he called. And you know me—I'm that guy who's always worried about everything.

"Even now, you know? Maybe especially now. I make everyone text me when they're home safe from having driven somewhere. Some of the guys at school who don't know me as well give me shit for it, but the guys who know about you know why I make them do it. It's like—my tiny way of doing what I can now, I guess. But I still feel like I'm not doing enough, even though I don't know what else I can be doing. I don't even know if there's anything else I can do.

"I guess I just wish I'd said something else to you before you left besides mumbling that I was going back to bed. I think I told you to drive safe. I think I told you I was glad we'd gotten to hang out that weekend. I don't remember the details, really. I just remember telling you I was heading straight back to bed after you left. You said that was the move, dapped me up, and you left.

"And that was it.

"I might have said bye again, I don't even remember. I went straight back up to my bed, collapsed into it, passed out within seconds. If your dad hadn't called, I'd a hundred percent have slept past noon.

"I'm sorry, man.

"I know, I know, I had no idea what would happen. Honestly, I think that's the worst part, you know? There are just so many what-ifs about what we probably would've done if you'd made it home and could've gone back to Vandy in the fall. Like, I'd have driven from Boston to Vandy for our annual visit. The last one of college, you know? Wouldn't have tried to beat your entrance, though. I remember you laughing at me sophomore year when I came to visit because you thought I was going to try and one-up you, but instead I just drove up and parked the car. Windows closed, one of our EDM playlists from high school playing at a medium volume. And you laughed at me.

"But I don't think I could have beaten your entrance if I'd tried, so I just didn't try. Dramatic entrances are always your thing. Honestly, no wonder you loved theater and singing so much. You got to own the stage.

"I guess you would've wanted a dramatic exit, too. You always blew a kiss when you were exiting after a performance with your a cappella group or whatever, and I always gave you shit for it, because I thought it was the funniest thing that you were this giant, burly dude who played hockey, but there you were blowing kisses at the audience and miming throwing roses, parading so delicately around that stage before disappearing behind the curtain. Everyone loved you. And honestly, even though I gave you shit for it, I thought it was great. I bet you know that, though.

"And, well, you definitely got a dramatic exit. Hit by an eighteen-wheeler, car totaled, gone on impact with pineapples rolling around in the freeway.

"And I barely even said goodbye."

*** 

A breeze sweeps across, catching the Frisbee on the other side of the river and sending it plunging toward the edge. One of the guys yells, chases it to the river's edge, and catches it, just barely, teetering on the edge of the grass as he fights to keep his balance. I seem to remember that happening to Ben and me, too, only I'm pretty sure I fell in the river instead, and it was Ben's turn to laugh his ass off as I held the Frisbee up over the surface, sopping wet but triumphant.

But I'm in Boston, not in DC, and I have an office to get back to. We get an hour for lunch.

I check my phone in my lap for the time. 12:32 PM. I have to be back by one. I've got texts from Jakub and Mom and a response from Dad, but I power down the screen and flip my phone over in my lap.

***

"Does it matter to you? I guess not. I feel like you probably know everything I think now. You know I love you, man. You know I'm sorry.

"Oh, man. I could've taken today off work, I guess, but I figured sitting at my apartment thinking about it would just make it worse. Plus, I could pretty much hear you yelling at me for not doing something with myself and just sitting around doing nothing and wallowing. So that's why I'm sitting under a tree by the Charles River, a five-minute walk from my office building. Looking like I'm talking to myself even though I have headphones in. Because I had to do something today, you know? I couldn't do something when that truck hit you, but I can sit here and talk to you now. It still doesn't feel like enough.

"Because honestly, even with anything I do for you now, I'd rather go back to the day you left my apartment and tell you to drive safe and to text me when you get there, even though I know you'd do both of those things. Tell you something other than a half-assed, half-asleep goodbye. Maybe it would delay you long enough for that truck to be ahead of you by the time you got on the road. Or go out there and push your car out of the way of that truck so I wouldn't have to be here, sitting under this tree, talking to you but not actually talking to you.

"Why did your car have to be part of that statistic, the one where you actually get killed? There are so many car accidents that people survive, and yours had to be the one that would kill you.

"It's harder, in a way. Because we're the ones who live with knowing what happened. Wishing we could have done something, you know?

"I can hear exactly what you'd say to me. 'Dude, you can't change that. Just focus on the things you can do now. Just remember me the way you want to.'

"God, you'd laugh if you saw me with no context. I'd never hear the end of it. But honestly, I'd shit myself if I saw you doing this and didn't know why, so I guess it goes both ways. But we both know the context, so no one's laughing.

"I'm glad I'm in Boston and not home in DC for the summer. That would be way too overwhelming. It's already hard enough with those two guys across the river right there.

"Every time I see pineapples at the grocery store, I get pissed, but I can't help laughing a little. Pineapples, man. It's funny. But you know, someone brought a fruit salad into work yesterday and left it in the break room for all of us, and there was pineapple in it, but I couldn't touch it. I just picked my way around those pieces and got watermelon and grapes and honeydew instead. Shana asked why I didn't take any pineapple, and I just told her I didn't like it and left it at that. I didn't want to get into it, really.

"Fucking pineapples, man."

***

I've run out of things to say, but I still feel heavy, as though the weight of my own words is flattening me as they hang in the air, unanswered. Wasn't I supposed to feel lighter? Wasn't that the whole point of why I came down here?

I snap the sticks at my feet in half and then in half again. The stiff cracks from the wood feel like they are releasing something poisonous, but I don't feel better, just empty.

Feeling stupid now, I chuck the pieces into the river, watch them as they bob on the surface and float away with the current, swirling lazily. Harmless.

I want to kick the tree, throw my hands up, scream at the sky. Anything to make this stop. Talking to Ben was supposed to make me feel better, not worse.

The sticks are caught in an eddy, swirling around each other by the riverbank.

I turn my back on the river, shove my phone in the pocket of my slacks, and start back toward the office, empty Tupperware in hand.

5.

# DON'T BURN OUT.

*Olivia, 20, Carmel Springs (MI, USA), 2018*
*"Time passes differently for each of us."*

Every morning when Olivia wakes up, she lights a sage and citrus Yankee jar candle on her nightstand and lets it burn while she gets ready. Sharp citrus and earthy sage swirl in the air, hitting her nose and the back of her throat. A hint of lavender drifts beneath it, slightly woodsy, like an afterthought.

Lighting the candle is the first part of her morning routine, whether she's home in Carmel Springs the way she is now or in her room at Penn State. While it burns, she washes her face, brushes her teeth, and then agonizes in front of her closet for twenty minutes trying to choose a sweater or a T-shirt or a dress, depending on what season it is. Sometimes, her fingers slide absently down the sleeve of his soft gray hoodie. Her brother's voice echoes in her ears.

"Come on, Olive, why do you want this one?" A teasing smile would tug at his lips, the one that always quirked up at the right corner when he didn't quite understand what she was on about. "I've had it since, like, high school. It doesn't even zip."

"It's nostalgic." She would always hug the hoodie to her chest, pull it tighter around her shoulders if she was wearing it. She stole it from him before he went to college. She couldn't get her brother's hugs while he was away, so the hoodie was the next best thing. "Plus, I like it. It reminds me of when you were young and clueless."

"Oh, fuck off." He'd give her a little push, but he'd be smiling, and she'd stick her tongue out at him even though she was sixteen and he was nineteen and they were both adults, sort of.

The memory drifts away on a wisp of candle smoke, and Olivia is back in her closet, trying to decide what to wear. Her fingers drift away from the hoodie, landing on a different shirt or sweater. It's always the top that takes her the longest to choose. Every morning when she does this, she wonders why she doesn't choose her clothes the night before. Whenever Colton used to ask her why she didn't, she never had a good answer.

Her phone gives a subtle buzz on her desk, telling her that she has five minutes before she has to leave for work and reminding her that she doesn't have time to lose herself in memories. She curses under her breath, pulls a shirt at random down from its hanger, and blows out the candle. She takes a moment to watch the candle smoke unfurl toward the ceiling, drifting in the air with the lingering sharp smells.

Olivia grabs her purse and pulls her dark blond hair into a ponytail as she walks out the door, pausing to grab a banana so she'll have something to eat on the way there. The house is already empty; Mom is leading a hike through the forest, and Dad's at his office. Sometimes, she still waits for Colton's shout from the back that she forgot something, but she knows it won't come.

Outside, the town of Carmel Springs is sleepy but warm, just stirring to life as she shuts the door behind her. She can practically hear Colton complaining about already feeling the midday humidity and wishing they were a beach town, not a lake town, so they could at least get a coastal breeze.

Her stomach still twinges faintly when she thinks about him, but really, it's okay.

\*\*\*

Marisa is worried. Not very, because Olivia is one of the strongest people she knows and it's been more than two years since Colton died, but she still wonders if the whole ordeal she watched her best friend go through has just been one sick, elaborate joke. She met Olivia on the first day of orientation at Penn, and she met Colton within the first week of knowing Olivia. They never became a trio—Colton was three years ahead of them, captain of the club tennis team, always busy—but he also always reserved a friendly hello for Marisa, always made time for Olivia. Marisa had known him, too.

Sometimes, it still feels like at any moment, Colton will come around the corner in the library mid-study session to mess up Olivia's hair until she swats him. He will throw Marisa a quick grin to say hello and turn back to Olivia to ask when they're getting dinner. When they were at Penn at the same time, Olivia and Colton made a point of getting dinner together at least once week.

Marisa knows this fantasy won't come to life, knows he won't come back. But sometimes, that little question prods at her, deep down, because she wasn't there when Colton died. She never saw it for herself. Marisa knows it's ridiculous, knows Olivia wouldn't ever lie about something as big as losing Colton, but she misses the way things were.

Marisa always liked watching Olivia and Colton with each other, because they didn't just look alike—dark blond hair, green eyes, tall and athletic—but they understood each other on a fundamental level that Marisa would never be able to match with her brother. When Olivia talks about Colton, Marisa always wonders what life might be like if she and Adrian had that sort of relationship. They are there for each other and they know it, but they're nothing like Olivia and Colton were.

And still, Marisa can't even begin to imagine what it would be like to lose Adrian. They have a mutual unspoken agreement that if one of them has a legitimate question, they will text each other. Even then, it's a once-a-week sort of deal. *What are you getting Mom for her birthday?*—Marisa, or *Did Dad send you money too?*—Adrian. They're not exciting texts, but she likes getting them. It's the closest she feels connected to him at school.

Marisa knows she doesn't talk about Adrian the same way Olivia talks about Colton, the way her friend's face softens and a slight smile tugs at her lips, the one that tugs slightly higher at the right corner in a way that's reserved just for him. Two years later, Marisa's best friend still slips into talking about her older brother in the present tense, something she's never quite been able to break herself of doing.

Once, Marisa asked her about it, eight months after Colton died. She remembers Olivia's right eyebrow arching, something it always did involuntarily when she was taken aback by a question. "He's still so present to me," she'd said, running a hand through her hair, making sure to meet Marisa's direct gaze with her own brown eyes. "I didn't really realize I was doing it until you said it."

Marisa had picked at one of her nails, wanting to ask the question but too nervous to look her friend in the eye. "Olivia, are you okay? You know you can talk to me about it, right?"

Olivia had nodded, a definitive bounce of her head that sent her long blond hair swishing. "Yeah, I do. But it's okay,

Marisa." A soft smile tugged at her lips, different than the one she reserved for talking about Colton. "I'm really doing okay."

"Are you sure?" Marisa had tilted her head to one side, raising an eyebrow at her best friend as though challenging her, but her heart was beating too quickly in her chest. These were uncharted waters for them. "I just want you to know that I'm here for you, you know? In any way you need."

"I know." Olivia smiled, but it was a brief flicker. "I do. But it's really fine. I've talked to my family about him; we're all dealing with it together."

Marisa wanted to tell Olivia how worried she was that her friend wasn't processing her brother's death. Her best friend was a closed book at the best of times, but she'd been truly impossible to read since Colton died, resolutely stoic since returning from the funeral eight months ago. She moved normally through her days, getting up and going to class and doing homework and throwing herself back into life at Penn as usual. Marisa had yet to see Olivia lose her cool about Colton's death, and it was scaring her, because she didn't know when those emotions could boil over. Surely, a breakdown was inevitable. She'd watched her mother go through it; Olivia would have to come to grips with it at some point.

Except she didn't.

Marisa hated feeling helpless, hated not knowing what to do and tiptoeing on eggshells because of it. Usually, she wouldn't mind telling Olivia what she was thinking; Olivia wouldn't care, because she'd seen Marisa at her worst. Now, Marisa couldn't tell if her friend was fragile and doing an excellent job of hiding it, or if nothing had really changed except for the fact that Colton was dead.

Instead, Marisa had nodded and smiled and moved on from the subject, because Olivia had that steely edge to her voice that she gets whenever she's signaling she wants to change the topic.

"You good over there?"

Marisa blinks, and she's back in the present, in the Mini Cooper with Jesse—it's early days, but she feels good about him—and they're most of the way through a road trip from Pennsylvania to Michigan to visit Olivia. He's driving, so he can't really look at her, but she can tell he's waiting for a response.

"Yeah. Yeah, I'm good." Marisa picks at the hem of her T-shirt. "It's just every time I see her here, it always reminds me of her and Colton. It's probably so hard coming back to Carmel Springs."

"Well, she's been doing it every year." Jesse's eyes shift as he changes lanes. "And anyway, it's not like she has much of a choice."

"Yeah, I guess." Marisa folds her arms over her chest to stop herself from pulling the hem of her T-shirt apart, remembering late nights in her bedroom wrapped in Olivia's embrace while down the hall, Marisa's mother drifted in space.

\*\*\*

Framed puzzles adorn the walls and boxed ones lean on stands on shelves as usual, and Olivia pauses to readjust a stack of boxes on a shelf before moving to the counter. The puzzle store smells like cedarwood and pine, with faint notes of sharp citrus and soft vanilla—remnants from yesterday at work. Four years ago, when Olivia was a junior in high school and Colton was in his sophomore year at Penn, Dad had first asked her to help out at the store for the summer, and she'd asked Colton to help her choose the candles.

"I love that you're doing this," Colton said, glancing sidelong at her from a few steps away, further down the shelf. "Makes me realize you actually miss me when I'm at school."

"Oh, shut up." Olivia threatened to lob a candle at him, and Colton flinched away, but she knew he could see the grin on her face.

"What about this one?" Colton held out a large Yankee candle jar, popped the lid off.

Olivia turned the jar over in her hands to read the label and brought the candle to her nose. "Balsam and cedar?" The woodsy smell of cedarwood and pine hit her nose, with a hint of sharp citrus and softer vanilla beneath. "I'm getting rustic store vibes from this one."

Colton raised an eyebrow at her, and Olivia grinned. "Right. I see your point."

"Here, let's grab a couple more." Colton stacked another three in his hands. "If you get enough, you'll get the whole store smelling like the woods."

"It's wax."

"Yeah, and? The store's on the lake, but the woods are on the other side. You can't smell the woods from the dock."

Olivia rolled her eyes, but she followed Colton's lead and added two more candles to the stack.

Now, Olivia stashes her bag under the counter and clips the store keys to the belt loop of her jeans. The puzzle store is usually quiet until the tourists emerge for the day, and even then it's rarely bustling. In between helping customers, she's started a puzzle on the table behind the counter, a 1,000-piece jigsaw of the lake Carmel Springs sits on. Colton took the picture that formed the basis of the puzzle out of his bedroom window. When Dad saw it, he immediately asked to borrow it for a puzzle. "It's perfect for a local puzzle store," he'd said. "It'll bring tourists back here."

"Just make sure you put my name on the photo at least," Colton had said. "I want my credit, after all."

"Of course, of course," Dad said, and when he came out with the puzzle, it had Colton's signature on the corner.

Olivia runs her hands over the pieces on the table, flips a few over in the hopes of finding something other than blue sky or lake. She's itching to get started, but she has something to do first.

Lighting the candles is part of her routine when she comes in to open the store, just like blowing out the candles and watching the smoke unfurl toward the ceiling is part of her routine when she closes. She reaches for the matchbox under the counter and strikes one to light the balsam and cedar candles placed around the store. She likes to watch the wick catch and the wax start to melt down to liquid as she moves from candle to candle, the mesmerizing flicker of candle fire as the tiny flame darts back and forth.

\*\*\*

"Look how pretty that is," Colton said, pointing at the candle on his desk. As the air around it moved, the flame flickered, darting back and forth.

Olivia was fifteen, home in Carmel Springs, sitting on the edge of Colton's bed with her legs swinging. "Have you always had a candle, or have I just noticed it?"

"Not really. I started getting them sophomore year when I realized they helped me stay calm when I'm stressed about work." Colton held out a hand. "Come here. Smell it."

Olivia held her blond hair back with one hand, put her face close to the candle, and drew a long breath. "A little citrusy. Lavender and a little bit of wood, too. Is that an herb? I can't tell what it is."

"Sage and citrus. Nice job." Colton held out a fist for her to pound, and Olivia bumped it with a smile. Colton was always great, but Olivia liked hearing him say she'd done a good job with something, even if it was about something as small as identifying the smell of a candle. "You want one?"

Olivia closed her eyes and breathed in the smell. Sharp citrus and earthy sage hit the back of her throat, but the heady scent seemed to settle in her veins, slowing her movements and soothing nerves about school she hadn't realized she had. "Yeah, that would be nice."

Colton grinned. "Christmas gift."

"I can't believe I didn't know you had these." Olivia dropped back on the bed, leaned back on one elbow.

"Yeah, I've been getting them for months," Colton said. "I was stressed all the time between tennis and school, and I was constantly Googling things trying to figure out how I could be less stressed. It took forever to find something that would work, and then one website suggested I try scented candles, which did work, so here we are." He gestured vaguely at the candle burning on his desk, the tiny flame whipping to one side with the breeze from his arm. "Get the big ones, though. Saves you money because it takes them forever to burn."

"I'm not even making money yet, so I don't have much to lose."

"That's true, I forget that sometimes." Colton smiled. Once he turned sixteen and started needing extra money, Dad let him help out at the puzzle store during the summer and after school. "Maybe Dad will let you work at the puzzle store next year."

"That would be nice." Olivia leaned back on her other elbow. "I could use the extra cash. I feel like it would be nice to stop making you pay for my dinner whenever we decide to go out."

"Ask him. When you're legally allowed to work, obviously. And you can't make me stop buying you dinner, Olive." Colton grinned at her, reached for the earphones on his desk. "All right. I hate to kick you out, but I really need to finish this essay, because it's due tomorrow and I have no idea what I'm doing."

"Yeah, that's okay, I should do work too." Olivia slid off the bed. "Later, Colt."

"Later, Olive. I'll take you to dinner this weekend. Do me a favor and order something other than the pesto this time."

"I make no promises."

"Guess you're not getting a Christmas gift, then."

"Hilarious." Olivia smiled as Colton's bedroom door clicked shut behind her. The Christmas gift threat was always an empty one.

On Christmas morning two months later, Olivia unwrapped a heavy rectangular box from Colton and lifted out a large Yankee candle jar with a sage and citrus label, and a smile tugged at her lips as her brother threw her a wink and a sly grin.

\*\*\*

The bell over the door of the puzzle store rings, and Olivia looks up from the table where she's trying to fit three blue pieces out of hundreds into the lake. Marisa's black head appears over the counter, accompanied by a friendly, attractive male face. Blue eyes, dark brown hair, straight nose. He looks vaguely familiar, but Olivia can't quite place him.

"Hey, Liv." Marisa folds her arms on the countertop. "Smells good in here."

"Yeah, Colton helped me pick those candles a while back, and I still use them. Can't seem to break the habit." Olivia smiles and abandons her jigsaw of the lake to step around the counter and talk to her best friend. "But more importantly, I thought you were coming tomorrow!" She wraps Marisa in a tight hug, breathing in the smell of her friend's argan oil shampoo before stepping back.

"Well, I got permission from my boss to work remotely, so I did a few things this morning before we drove up. I wanted to surprise you." Marisa runs a hand through her black hair. "Which reminds me, Olivia, this is Jesse, and Jesse, this is Olivia. She's my best friend from Penn."

Olivia smiles as she shakes Jesse's hand; she remembers Marisa mentioning him but not in the capacity of him driving her all the way to Michigan. "Nice to meet you."

"You too." Jesse's voice is pleasant, a deep rumble in his chest, and as his eyes wander around the puzzle store, Olivia shoots Marisa a look—raised eyebrows and a suppressed grin—to which her best friend rolls her eyes, but there's a suspicious grin tugging at the left corner of her lips.

"You work here?" Jesse asks, pulling Olivia's attention away from her evasive best friend.

"It's my dad's store, so I'm indulging in nepotism to make some extra cash before senior year." Olivia smiles.

"Nice." Jesse's looking around at the boxes and the framed puzzles on the walls, but his hand stretches slowly out to Marisa's, and Olivia tries to hide a smile as their fingers intertwine. Yet his eyes turn back to Olivia's, an alertness in his expression, as though he's suddenly recognized her. "You're Colton's little sister, aren't you?"

Olivia tilts her head, a frown tugging her brows together. "Yeah, why?"

"I was his year at Penn," Jesse says. "We had a lot of classes together, so we were sort of friends. Really sucks, what happened to him. I'm sorry."

"Thank you." Olivia gives him a soft smile because what else can she do? "It's not necessary, but thanks."

Out of the corner of her eye, she sees Marisa giving her a look. One eyebrow arched, corner of her mouth screwed to one side. Olivia knows that look. Her best friend is scrutinizing her, the way she always does when Olivia talks about Colton.

"He talked about you all the time." Jesse grins. "He thought you were pretty cool."

Olivia smiles. "Well, that's always good to hear. He'd always tease me that he was painting the worst picture of me in front of his friends, like I was this completely crazy, wild kid. Except then he'd drop the act and say, 'No, they think you're pretty cool.' Said they thought it was cool that we're so close."

"I bet you miss him."

"Oh, I do." Olivia doesn't miss Marisa's tiny exhale, but she decides not to acknowledge it. Not in front of Jesse, anyway. "But it's really okay." She gestures to the candles all around her, the jigsaw on the table. "In a way, it's almost like he's still here."

"You talk about him like that a lot," Marisa says, and Olivia glances around to see her friend inspecting the puzzle she's working on at the table.

"Yeah, well." Olivia draws a breath and reminds herself to keep her expression neutral. She knows what Marisa's trying to do, what she's been trying to get Olivia to do for the past three years. "Even though he's gone, he's still my brother, you know?"

"Yeah, of course," Jesse is quick to answer.

"Yeah," Marisa says, after too long of a pause.

Olivia doesn't want to be mad at Marisa, because her best friend is only trying to help and to understand, but she wishes Marisa would make her feel less guilty about the way she has spent the past three years honoring her brother. Olivia knows she's okay, and she's been trying to get Marisa to see it, but she hasn't succeeded just yet.

She knows Marisa's concern comes from experience. Olivia remembers the weekends at Marisa's house after her best friend's grandmother died and her mother wouldn't come out of her room unless it was to go to work. It was the same year that Colton died. She remembers keeping Marisa's younger brother and sisters entertained with books and games while Marisa made dinner and hid her tears until the kids were in bed and it was just the two of them.

Olivia knows that Marisa's brush with death is an experience that will never leave her, of watching her loved one come apart before her eyes and having to pull her back from space. Of having to put her back together, piece by piece until she's whole again.

\*\*\*

Olivia was eighteen, the younger one, but somehow, she was supposed to be the strong one for both of them when Colton had always been that for her. His grasp was loose in her hand as she sat by his bedside, her eyes on his face. She was used to the many tubes and wires now. She had known, when he sat her down a year ago to tell her about the lymphoma, that it was going to be a long, uphill battle with a dwindling chance of recovery each time the cancer came back. She had known she would have to learn how to be strong for both of them.

But she still didn't know how to do that, even though she thought she should now that it was almost time for Colton to leave her.

"Don't wallow, Olivia, okay?" Colton's voice was creaky now, with the exhaustion of simply existing to hold on, but he was being serious. It was one of the few times he'd ever called her Olivia.

Olivia chewed on her lower lip, managing a tiny smile. "What makes you think I'd be wallowing?"

Colton, too, managed a tiny smile, the corners of his lips tugging up just enough so that the right corner pulled a little higher than the left. "That's my girl."

Olivia watched the slight rise and fall of his chest, found herself counting the breaths, wondering which one would be the last. Wondering how her big brother, once the star tennis player of their high school and captain of the club team at Penn, a few months away from graduating, could have been reduced to a shell of his former self, skin almost translucent.

"Balsam and cedar for the store, sage and citrus for the house. Don't you forget it."

Olivia squeezed his hand. "Colt, that's been the routine for the past three years."

"Yeah, I know," Colton's smile widened into a grin. "Just making sure you remember."

"Bold of you to assume I'd forget."

"You're right." Colton's grip on her hand softened a little. "There's a stash in my room, if you're ever looking for more."

"Where?"

"Closet. There's a box on the top shelf. Sage and citrus."

"Don't tell me you've got a stash in the store too."

"Okay, I won't." Colton's eyes had fluttered shut, but that grin was still tugging at his lips.

Olivia sat up. "No. Where?"

"Back room. You get to figure out where that box is, though."

Olivia's eyes widened. "Dad keeps so many boxes back there."

Colton's eyes fluttered back open, and his grin widened. "Exactly."

The door to Colton's room in the hospital creaked open, and Olivia looked up to see Mom and Dad following the nurses into the room. The moment was lost.

Olivia went back to school a week after Colton died. There was no point in staying home. *"Don't wallow, Olivia, okay?"*

She posted a tribute to him on Instagram right before the three-hour drive so she could avoid obsessing over the notifications for a few hours. He would have done the same for her.

When she got back to campus, she had four hundred likes and over thirty comments. Olivia had always been glad Instagram had introduced the feature to like comments, because it meant she could acknowledge them without answering. Something about the number of condolence comments and texts coming from even mere acquaintances, like the girl she'd only had one class with first year, made her feel better because she knew it was what Colton would have done if the same thing happened to someone he barely knew.

His friend Evan texted her a funny story about the time he and Colton had stolen one of the banners from one of the football games when no one was looking, and when Olivia said she'd laughed out loud at that story because it was Colton who had insisted on stealing it when he was usually such a rule-follower, the floodgates opened with texts, some from people she didn't even remember Colton mentioning. Stories about long drives just to unwind, spontaneous trips to New York; a story about breaking into one of the frat houses to steal their 'Saturdays are for the Boys' flag. She got over thirty texts with stories about Colton in that one day. She'd heard a few of them already, but she liked getting a laugh out of it.

That night in her dorm, Olivia covered the smoke detector with tape, lit a sage and citrus candle, and lay on her bed with her eyes closed as the sharp scents swirled together in the air, remembering her brother healthy at eighteen and the sly grin on his face as she unwrapped a sage and citrus candle next to a heavily decorated tree on Christmas morning. She tried to think about which of the boxes in the back of the store held the candle stash he was talking about. It made her chest hurt and her eyes sting, but she knew he was in a better place now, still watching her. *"We already said our goodbyes, Olivia, what are you lying around for?"*

The door opened, and Olivia lifted her head from her bed to see Marisa coming in with her backpack and her dark hair in a high ponytail on top of her head. They were already each other's best friend at Penn despite only meeting this year, matched as roommates thanks to the randomizing system. They lived well together, had similar clothing tastes, and loved to watch hockey together, but they were also very different. Marisa liked to share, to talk things through to understand them even if she had already been through the issue dozens of times. Olivia liked to talk to Marisa, but she was not a big talker when it came to herself. She liked to deal with things on her own.

The slight wrinkle between Marisa's eyebrows as the door shut behind her already told Olivia she was going to get an earful she didn't need, and she dropped her head back on to her pillow.

"Hey." Marisa's voice was so soft that Olivia could hear the hesitation in the back of her throat.

"Hey, what's up?"

"Are—are you okay?"

Olivia sat up so that Marisa could see her face and know she was telling the truth. "Yeah, I'm all right." She frowned slightly and then said, "I mean, obviously it sucks, but I'm okay."

Marisa's frown deepened. "Really—I mean, okay."

"I had some time at home with family to deal with it, and I mean, we all knew it was coming. So we got to say our goodbyes, close that chapter out properly." Olivia kept her voice quiet. "So really, I'm okay with it."

"Are you—okay, if you're sure."

Olivia offered her best friend a soft smile. "I promise you, if I need anything I can't get from my parents, you'll be the first to know."

\*\*\*

"What are you thinking?" Marisa's voice is soft.

Olivia glances sidelong at her best friend, sitting next to her on the dock with her black hair in a high ponytail, feet hanging over the glossy surface of the lake. Dad dropped by the store a few moments ago and ran into Jesse, who started talking about Colton, so Olivia had glanced at her dad, pointed at the back door, and grabbed Marisa's arm when he nodded. "Just that it's nice to be home."

"You miss him?"

"Of course." Olivia rests her hands on the sun-warmed dock behind her, tips her head back so that the sun hits her cheeks. "But, you know, even though he's gone, and I know that, I still feel like he's here. Because I carry him every day, you know?"

"Yeah. Yeah, that makes sense." Marisa glances over her shoulder. "I guess I just couldn't always tell."

"I think we just process things differently." Olivia offers her friend a slight smile, but she can hear the prickly edge to her own voice. "Which isn't a bad thing, you know? It just means we understand death differently."

Marisa considers the point with her head slightly to one side. "Yeah, that's true. I guess I never thought of it that way." A short laugh escapes her, almost a huff. "Three years later and I never thought of it like that. Guess that shows you where I'm at."

Olivia lets the silence stretch, sensing that Marisa is gathering herself to say more.

"I guess I just thought you would be in the same place as me," Marisa says. "But maybe that's stupid because we're totally different people. It makes sense that Colton meant something different to you than my grandma did to me."

"Yeah." Olivia doesn't look at Marisa, because if she does, she will lose her nerve, and she needs to tell her friend what she's been thinking. "I've been trying to get you to see that for a really long time."

Silence hangs in the air between them, heavy and loud, before Marisa finally says, "I'm sorry I didn't see it sooner."

# 6.

# RESOLUTION...

*Zoey, 32, Palo Alto (CA, USA), 2004*
*"What do you do with the hand you've been dealt?"*

Zoey twitches her fingers in her lap and looks up at the ceiling. She starts to count the white tiles as she breathes in, out. The door to her left has a nameplate. *Dr. Max Akim, PhD*. It is still closed.

Six, seven.

The doorknob turns, and Zoey bolts to her feet as the door to her left swings open and Dr. Akim, PhD, gestures for her to come in, a warm smile on his face. She can just see a couch from where she's standing but not one of those stereotypical lounge couches from a psychologist's office in a movie. A nice one, navy blue. If she weren't in an office building, she could see it in someone's apartment.

\*\*\*

"I'm kind of nervous. I'm not used to talking about this, all at once."

"No, don't take it personally. It's not you."

"Well, I'm just not used to laying the whole story out, all the losses, all the sadness. I've talked about each one, of course—I think it's healthier to talk when you need to—but I've never strung them together in this way. But I've felt a tug to tell the whole story recently, and I think that's what led me here, to your office. I'm just having trouble getting started."

"Yes, I'm comfortable. Thank you for asking. I like the view from here, too. I'm just really nervous."

"Well, I'm just not sure what the easiest place to start would be."

"The first thing I think of—I mean, I used to tell myself it would get easier. That's how you learn something is supposed to work, isn't it? You keep doing something over and over again and eventually, it gets easier."

"I mean, no, I haven't found that's true. That's the point I'm trying to make. It doesn't get easier, even with God's grace."

"The first time I learned about death? Well, I don't really remember it, because I was four. It was my grandmother who passed away."

"I mean, I remember my mom telling me that Granny was dead, but as a four-year-old, you don't really understand what death is, or anything like that, but your mom sure does."

"She coped with her faith. It was her lifeline. My mom is the one who taught me about God, even at that young age."

"I mean, I grew up in a house that put God at its center. So when Granny died, my mom was always reassuring me, saying things like, 'Zoey, honey, it's okay. We prayed every day that Granny would go quietly, painlessly, remember? And God heard our prayers, and He took her in her sleep.'"

"I mean, I guess it helped, because Mom was saying it was okay, so I thought it was okay. And it helped to have something to hold on to, something to believe in. But when I was four, I didn't really understand what 'going' like that meant, you know? I did remember praying with my parents that if Granny had to go, it would be quiet and painless, and it was. That was the first time I experienced death. A gentle introduction, if you will."

"Why gentle? I don't know. I've always thought that it was Mom and God protecting me from the harsh realities that death can bring, because I was four and I was too little to understand what could go wrong in the world just yet. I guess that's what I mean by 'gentle.'"

"Right, the second time. Well, I was older by that point, I think twelve. I was lucky enough to be spared the reality of grieving the first time; I know my mom prayed that I wouldn't have to try to grapple with grief until I was old enough to understand it with God's help. I think she believed it would be easier for me to understand once I got older."

"I'm not sure if it was really easier to understand. I think it helped to know what I was experiencing, but I don't think that knowing I was experiencing grief made it easier to deal with, if that makes sense. What helps me is to know that God has a plan, that everything happening is part of His plan for my life, even if it hurts."

"I try not to question God's plan, but sometimes it's hard."

"Well, sometimes you have to wonder why this has to be your plan. I would catch myself wondering why His plan requires me to lose so many people I love, but I keep reminding myself that I can't doubt His reasons. I don't know those reasons yet, but I pray every day that I will find them out soon."

\*\*\*

Zoey drops her gaze, fiddles with one of the ends of her snatched black braids. Turns to the window, to the view of the street below. Starts to count the cars that are passing by.

Four, five.

Across from her, Dr. Akim, PhD, shifts in his chair and leans forward.

Zoey turns her gaze back to him, brown eyes shrewd and bright in the dark skin of his face, and draws a breath.

***

"Yes, the second time. I'm sorry; I can feel myself stalling."

"I think I'm stalling because I just don't talk about Lily's death very often. When she died, it really rattled me. I think it was when I properly learned what it was to lose someone I know I love and to have to grieve."

"Well, I say that because I was twelve. And at twelve, you don't understand everything, but you know what death is, and you understand that it's permanent. But you're still so young, really, that it's scarier to have your world turned upside-down that way when you don't see it coming."

"I was close with this lovely girl Jess—it wasn't her, though, I'm still friends with her to this day. Jess and I met in kindergarten, so we were often over at each other's houses, so we knew each other's families very well too. Lily was one of Jess's older sisters. Hannah was the other. Hannah was the oldest one; she was already in college at Santa Clara, so we didn't get to see much of her, but Lily was only three years older than us, and she was always very sweet and hung out with us like we were her age, even though we were younger and not always the 'coolest' kids."

"Well, when Jess and I were twelve, Lily was in a van accident. She played tennis for her high school, and they were on their way to a game. There was another car, and the driver was texting and didn't see their van, so they T-boned."

"I'm sorry. I just need a second."

"Thank you for letting me take my time with this. I'm sorry, I didn't expect to get this emotional talking about it, though I suppose I should have expected that, since I don't talk about it much. But I guess that's one thing that got easier—the talking about it, I mean."

"I think it got easier just because you find ways to talk about death that aren't so heart-wrenching. But, you know, I haven't talked about this one as much, so I still haven't figured it out."

"Well, Lily survived the initial crash, but there were some complications with her injuries—a lot of internal bleeding and bone fragments—and she stayed in a coma for about a week before her parents decided it would be kinder to take her off life support. And Jess and her family were incredible. They stayed so strong through the whole ordeal—the funeral, the aftermath, and putting the pieces back together. If they were shattered, they didn't show it."

"I mean, for me, it really shook me up, losing someone so close to my own age that I knew well, you see?"

"I didn't do much about it, really. When I told my mom about it, she said it was God's plan for Lily, and we prayed for her. She was only meant to have fifteen years on this earth, and God knew what He was doing, even when He took her away from us."

"I mean, I felt secure, knowing that God was now protecting Lily and that she was at peace in heaven where God and her grandparents were taking care of her, but I was starting to ask questions. Not about God—I know that He plans everything for us for a reason, and one day, we learn that reason—but about why that had to be Lily's plan. Does that make sense? My faith in Him never wavered once, but I always wondered, a little, why He had chosen that path for Lily."

"Yes, I did ask Jess about it, once. Her family doesn't believe in God, and that was the first time I really learned about other ways people cope with death. That time marked a lot of firsts, I'm realizing now. Maybe that's why I don't talk about it much."

"Sorry, I've lost track again. Where was I?"

"Ah yes. Well, Jess and her family believe in Buddhist principles, in reincarnation and rebirth after death. They believed they would find Lily's spirit again, that it would seek out someone they would meet in life when they needed her most."

"I mean, I was a little skeptical, I guess. I feel so close to God that it's difficult to believe there's anyone other than Him determining what happens to us. I still believe Lily is in heaven and that I'll see her up there when it's my time. But I do think there's something to be said about the way believing in God or reincarnation or other faiths that are out there can help a person when they lose someone they love."

"For me? I think for me, God took Lily to show me that there are other ways of coping that can help people. Not everyone believes in Him, but as long as they have something to help them through, that's okay. And that was nice to see, as a twelve-year-old."

"I don't know why it was so nice. I think it was just because I really wanted to be helpful, even though I didn't know how, and at the same time, I was also trying to figure out grieving for Lily. So even though my faith couldn't help them, they had something that could. And that opened my mind, I think, in a way that learning about it from books just couldn't really do for me. Their conviction really sealed it. Jess and her family really believed that they would find Lily's spirit in the world again, somewhere, when the time was right, and that was their lifeline in the months after she died."

"Well, that's the crazy thing. When Jess started university—she went to Howard University, in DC—she started tutoring kids at a school in the area, and she told me got paired with a little girl who looked exactly like Lily and who had so many of Lily's little mannerisms. Jess said it was like she'd found her sister again."

\*\*\*

Zoey folds her hands in her lap. Looks back out the window. On the street below, a red Kia Soul is passing by, like the one Jess used to drive.

She draws a deep breath and turns back to the room. Her gaze fastens on the jade plant on a table in the back. Jade, for luck.

\*\*\*

"I guess it's hard to talk about because it's the first time I started to question why God would plan to take someone away at such a young age, especially when they have all these aspirations for themselves. And that's a difficult thing to admit, you know?"

"Oh, no, I'm not questioning God. I'm not questioning that God has a plan, either. I just want to know why He made it this way, so that I can truly rest with the decision, but I still don't know the answer. I take comfort in what I believe—that Lily is in heaven—but it bothered me that I didn't really know why she had to leave. I hope that makes sense."

"Well, I'm coming to that. I thought about Lily and I prayed for her every day, even though I could feel that she was at peace in heaven. It was just my little thing I did to honor her every day. I prayed that she had found happiness in heaven and that I could someday know that she was watching over us all. At the same time, I was applying to colleges, and I was looking at ones where I could really challenge myself. I was always interested in environmental science, and as I got older and it became more important with the warning signs of climate change, I knew it was a sign that it was my time to study this and do something good for the world and for our planet."

"I applied to schools in the States that I knew had rigorous environmental science programs—Pomona, Taylor, and the University of Hawaii at Hilo—but where I really wanted to study was the University of Lausanne, because even though it was across the country and the Atlantic, it had a really great program for environmental studies, I'm fluent in French, and I had always wanted to go to Switzerland. I knew it as one of the greenest and most beautiful countries in the world."

"And here's how it connects to Lily: she and Jess and I had always talked about what we wanted to do with our futures. Lily and I both wanted to study environmental science, even at different ages, but we didn't talk about universities when I was twelve. After she passed away, I was even more determined to pursue it, both in her honor and for the fact that the need for climate change solutions was intensifying. And while I prayed for Lily, I prayed that I would get into Lausanne. And God heard my prayers, and He answered: I got in. But it also felt like a sign from Lily, like her blessing that I was meant for this. And I knew, when I got my acceptance letter, that even if I never knew why she had died, I was going to complete the journey she had started, because when I got in, Jess and her mother both revealed to me, separately, that Lily had wanted to go to the University of Lausanne to study environmental science, too."

"I think that question will remain unresolved for a long time. But because I know to follow on her path, I'm okay to live with that, even though sometimes, it still bothers me."

"Yes, the third time. I know I'm getting a bit off the rails, but as I said, I'm not used to telling the story all in one go. The third time was very much out of nowhere. My last year at Lausanne, my mother had a sudden heart attack, and she died just minutes after, before they could even get her into the hospital for any kind of surgery. I barely even had time to pray that God could save her and that if He couldn't, to show her some kindness. She died maybe a few minutes after that."

"I have to admit, it did shake me, a little. It was the first time a concrete prayer of mine had gone unanswered, and the question of why that happened haunted me for months afterward as I wrestled with my faith and with death. But I knew that one, my mother would tell me that it was always God's plan for her, and two, that I couldn't let losing my mother, who had taught me to believe in God, rattle my faith."

"I mean, of course, it was difficult. The more people you lose, the more you wonder why it keeps happening, why God is planning for you to lose all of the people around you. Granny, and then Lily, and now my mother. I told myself that my mother had always prayed that when it was her time, she would go quickly, and she did. So, at least, her prayer was answered."

"I guess it changed my understanding a little bit. Sometimes, when God has a plan, a prayer can't change it. To die quickly was my mother's wish for herself, and God granted it to her. And later, when I was a little more removed from the immediacy of it, I remembered praying that if the doctors couldn't save her, she would go quickly, the way she always wanted to. So, in the end, God had answered my prayers after all."

"Sometimes, I wonder if she suffered, even though it was quick, but that's a question I won't get answered for a long time."

***

Zoey draws a long breath and reaches for the glass next to her for a few sips of water. She had forgotten what it was like to really talk. But there is something about the quiet presence of Dr. Akim, PhD, that draws her words out, pulling thoughts from beneath the surface and turning them into elegant, twisted sentences that build her story. That are just starting to make it make sense.

***

"The thing is, the year after my mother's death was the most difficult of my life and not even because of the aftermath of losing her. I lost three more people in the span of a year. One of my good friends at university took his own life, and then my father died—after my mother died, he was never quite right—and then another one of my friends had complications with pneumonia and she just couldn't recover. And the more funerals you attend, the more you start to wonder, why did God plan this for all of them? Especially my friends, who were my age. How did they get dealt such a bad hand, and how come I remain behind?"

"I mean, I used to ask myself that question all the time—the 'why am I here when they aren't' kind of thing. It's impossible not to think about that when the circles around you grow smaller and smaller. But I think that because of those losses, my friends and I are close in a way that most groups of friends are not. We cried together, we shared our beliefs about life after death with each other, we shared all our questions and the web of emotions that catches you in grief. We still grieve together, and we're closer for it, I think."

"I made sure we talked about it. I've always thought it's healthier to talk about it than to keep it inside, especially if you *want* to talk about it. It helps, to put things into words, I think. After Steven and Liza died, one of the friends from that circle, Tuli, told me she was really grateful to have someone to talk to, because her family wasn't closely connected in a way where she was comfortable talking to them about those losses. And in a twisted sort of way, it was nice to know that my friends and I were going through this together, so we could talk openly about it and we were able to lean on each other. It was an awful year, because there was just so much to have to recover from, but we had to move forward. Every day when I woke up, I thanked God that I was still here, on this earth, and I asked for more time so that I could stay to help my friends some more. He has always been kind to me."

"I guess I think of it as twisted because there's a sort of irony to it. The idea that losing two of our friends is what brought us closer together."

"Oh, no, of course I'm grateful for my friends and that none of us had to go through that alone. God blessed me with a truly amazing support system. I've just always thought that it was a little sad, how loss tends to bring people closer together. But I suppose that's the blessing of having a such a great support system. You know you're never alone. And I remind them of that, every day, that we always have each other. We're lucky that way, to have that support system of friends around us. But I also know that even among all this loss, God is holding my hand, and He is guiding me toward my purpose. Not everyone is lucky enough to have something to believe in or someone to hold on to in the aftermath of a loss."

"Yes, I'm coming to that. I'm still not sure what my purpose is. And I think that maybe, beyond the need to tell this story, that is the reason I'm here. With so much loss, I spend so much time grieving that I think I'm losing track of what it is I need to do in life, but I also think the two are connected. I can't abandon the path that Lily started, and I do love the work I do. I work on marine conservation on the Pacific Coast. But I'm restless. I'm starting to feel like somewhere, in the tangled lines that make up my story, God is pointing me to my purpose, and I have to discover what it is. So here I am, trying to discover it."

"I think so. I think it's a good message to spread. Communication and talking are important, whether you are speaking to God or to your friends or to something or someone else that helps you believe. It helps, to talk out loud."

\*\*\*

Zoey sits back in her chair, draws a long breath, and offers Dr. Akim, PhD, a tentative smile, thanking him for listening, even though she's not done yet.

He returns it, warm, inviting. Thanking her for sharing.

\*\*\*

"It was helpful, to share the whole story from start to finish. I've never done that before today, because it's always been written for me as I was living it. It's only because it's been ten years since Steven and Liza and my father died, and the losses have slowed down for me, that the questions have started nagging at me again. And I know everyone I have lost—Lily, Steven, Liza, my parents, and I'm sure Granny as well—they would tell me to do something about it. But I've never tried, because I've never been quite sure what to do."

"Oh, that's such a great idea! It might sound weird that I'd never considered it before, but I've truly never thought about expanding beyond my circle of friends. Which is funny, when you think about it, because I've been talking about how much I think talking can help people. But maybe I wasn't ready yet, until I came here and gave it a real try myself."

"I love that idea. Thank you. I'll think on it some more, but I love that I have something I can move toward now."

"Ten minutes left? I didn't realize time had gone by so quickly."

"Other questions… I guess I've always wondered if after this many losses, I'm supposed to have formed some sort of philosophy on it by now. On the process."

"I mean, losing each of them felt a little different. I did different things for each of them when they passed. I keep them all in my prayers, of course. I hardly remember Granny and that experience, so that's about all I can think to do for her. But for Lily, obviously, there's environmental science, and Jess and I always do something together around her anniversary or birthday, depending on what's easiest for each of us. She spends those harder days with her family, of course. And then for Steven, I always try to find a body of water to sit by for a bit and just remember him. We always used to hang out by the lake in Lausanne. It's harder now that I'm back home and working. In Lausanne, I could just wander down to the lake after class. Now I drive down to the Bay on weekends, and it's a hike, but it's worth it. It's different, but it's still nice to have that space for him."

"I light two scented candles for my parents. They loved experimenting with different ones, so I really like finding ones I think they would have liked when I burn down the candles I've been using. My mother liked woodsy ones; my father liked the ones that had more herby smells. And Liza loved writing, so I always write her a letter on her anniversary, and then occasionally when I just want to tell her something. So I do different things for all of them. And they all feel right. But I think that's part of why I'm confused."

"That's true. Maybe it being different every time is part of the message. I'll have to think on that. But to go back to questions, wouldn't you think it would be time for me to arrive at a resolution of some kind for each of them? I pray every day that they rest peacefully, and I think that they do, but I still can't bring myself to let go of them."

"I don't know, exactly. I guess I'm afraid of forgetting about them. But at the same time, I know I could never. People always have their way of leaving a mark, you know? But sometimes, marks fade. And I don't want them to fade."

"That's true. I suppose this kind of mark is permanent. And I've always asked God that whatever else He takes from me, I will at least get to keep my memory, and I have. I think people are never really gone until you let yourself forget about them, and I could never let myself do that. But I still worry, a little bit."

"Is that our time? I'd love to come back. I've really enjoyed this conversation; it's given me so much to think about."

"It might be too early to tell if I feel different. But I feel good."

\*\*\*

As Zoey leaves the office and steps into the street, a smile tugs at her lips. The kind of smile she gets when she has a breakthrough in her research, the moment when her thoughts click together and the dots finally connect to fully sharpen the picture. She has some friends to call.

7.

# DEAR KELSEY,

*I've been trying to write something for you for over a year, ever since the morning of August 1, 2018, when I learned that you were gone. I think I've finally landed on the right thing. And I hope you don't mind that I've done this.*

*You see, I wanted to write for you because in a selfish sort of way, it helps me gather the words and put names to exactly what I'm going through so that I can settle down and process it. Everyone has to learn about death at some point, right? And I thought I sort of had, already, the year before, when my grandmother passed. But it turns out there was a whole other lesson to be learned.*

*And I didn't think I would start to learn it with you, didn't think it would start with a text when I was a full twenty-four-hour journey away from where you were. But that's the nature of the twenty-first century, isn't it? News travels fast and furiously, and in the end, I've come to realize that it was so much better to hear about it right away, even if it was over text, than it would have been to find out in person two weeks after the fact.*

*There's another thing, though. I wanted to write for you to make sure that I had done something you could be proud of. As your friend. Never mind that you were the kind of person who lived life with unconditional love, who was proud of your friends no matter how small their accomplishments, who encouraged positivity and humor and sparkle at every turn. I* think I wanted to give you something concrete. To feel that I had done something for you.

I hope I've done that.

Yet even now, almost two years, one essay, and a short story collection later, I still haven't managed one thing. I still don't have that perfect story to tell about you. I've been trying to land on one ever since I wrote that essay, and I haven't locked one down.

What I do have are dozens upon dozens of fragments of memories, scraps of images that come together to leave behind the last portrait of you I will have. The scrap of notebook paper you gave me seven-and-a-half years ago with your contact information that is still tucked away somewhere in my desk at home. Your unbridled love of Halloween, best encapsulated by your recounting of how painstakingly you went about pulling together the perfect mermaid costume so that you and your boyfriend, whose mother of all people insisted that he dress as a fisherman, would still be able to pull off a couple's costume. You, standing at the edge of Big Schloss, the mountain of our last hike of the summer of 2016, belting either "Circle of Life" or "Under the Sea" (I wish I remembered which) out to the trees to an interpretive dance that kept me and my fifteen cabinmates in stitches, and that I wish I could have captured in video instead of photos. You, veering way off the path and disappearing into the bushes during hikes so you could pick all the wild berries you could find and eat them on the way back to camp.

Our horse memories—our long conversations that would unwind late at night, most of them about our vision of the ideal horse stable for camp, which required way more money than camp would be able to afford and did not include about half the horses that were there. The good luck note and the horseshoe you spray painted gold and left on my bunk on the day of my last horse show as a camper, both of which now spend most of their time in my college dorm room. Our love of Longfellow, that gorgeous lanky ex-racehorse with a star and a snip and a habit of getting too excited when someone got in the saddle and asked him to do more than walk around in a circle, and the lesson plans we'd work through to calm him down. I always loved when I got to ride him and when you were teaching, because I watched you ride him once, and I knew we loved him and believed in him in the same way. The bear hug you gave me when I saw you at the camp horse show in July of 2018 for the first time in two years and the genuine joy that lit up your face, visible even behind your big sunglasses. The first thing you told me was how much my then fifteen-year-old sister Kanitta reminded you of me, because our voices sound so similar and because we have so many of the same mannerisms, and how much having her around made you miss me.

That last memory stings a little because it's the last one we'll ever make together. But I'm learning to accept it. And for the same reason, I treasure it.

\*\*\*

You know, I still don't know how it happened. I only know it was a riding accident, early in the morning, out on the trails. But I'm too afraid to ask someone which horse it was, what trail you were on, whether you were wearing a helmet. I don't want them to have to think about that day any more than they have to. The only person I would feel comfortable asking is you.

But I think that's okay. I don't think I need the details. It's not like it changes my portrait of you in any way. Maybe *someday, I'll feel brave enough to ask. For now, maybe for forever, it's enough to know that you died doing exactly what you loved most, in one of your favorite places on earth.*

*It sounds so corny but for anyone who knew you—who still knows you—we know how deeply true that is.*

*They will not stop the riding program at camp, and I'm glad they won't, because I know you would be devastated. Except for the young girls of nervous parents, everyone I know that knew you kept riding that summer and beyond. Their love for the horses, for this sport that has taught them so much, has not wavered. At least, not externally. I haven't asked them. I don't want to know if it has.*

*I'm sure you know this, but I haven't stopped riding since you fell. I literally looked for ways to ride while abroad in Geneva for part of the spring semester. Not being able to ride when I came home in the midst of the pandemic, despite being so close to my home barn, nearly drove me insane. And except for the little corrections that my coach asks of me, I haven't changed much about how I ride, either. Two weeks after August 1, 2018, I went to my home barn and led a public trail ride because my boss asked me to come in and help. I didn't even consider saying no.*

*When I slide my foot into the left stirrup and swing up, I think about how wonderful it is to settle into a leather saddle that has been broken in and cared for and loved. I reach forward to pat my horse's neck and watch his ears turn back to catch my voice or her head turn back to look at me, and I smile, because the moment of knowing a horse is actively, willingly listening to you is always magical, no matter how many times it happens.*

*I do not think about the things that could go wrong, about the chance that I could fall off or that my life could be permanently changed or taken away. I think about the work I have to put in to get my horse to do what I am asking, about that unique partnership that exists between horse and rider, about how much I love and trust these dangerous, beautiful creatures.*

*I do not think about the fact that a horse took your life away.*

*I wonder if it is because I am a rider that my approach to the sport hasn't changed since you fell. I am not afraid to ride bareback or take a horse out on the trails, alone or in a group. Because I know you would say that what happened to you was a freak accident. We risk one every time we put a foot into the stirrup and swing into the saddle. The odds are the same, no matter which horse we are riding. All it takes is one tumble, one misjudged takeoff or landing to a jump, one misstep by the horse to change or take a life.*

*I have always known this. Knowing how you left us doesn't change that risk. It doesn't change my love for the horses and people I have come to know from this sport. It doesn't change my love of settling into a well-worn leather saddle and letting everything melt away except for me and the horse. It doesn't change the fun we had when we rode at camp, or the fun I have when I ride at my barn at home.*

*So why would I give it all up?*

\*\*\*

*Your service was beautiful. I want you to know that. But I'm sure you already do.*

*On the evening of August 12, 2018, we gathered for what your family called a celebration of your life. They asked that everyone wear bright colors, and I know you would have loved that. A celebration is something happy, a time to wear bright colors and rejoice. Maybe your family knew that you wouldn't have wanted everyone to look as though they were mourning. Maybe you knew that the bright colors would make everything a little bit easier. It did make it easier, somehow, to see everyone clad in bright floral prints, in bright greens and pinks and blues instead of the soft blacks and grays I'm sure everyone would have worn if they hadn't expressly been told not to. As a color, you would have been a splash of brightness, a deep swirl from across the spectrum of bright colors that clashed wildly but still, somehow, worked together in harmony. Maybe your family knew that to have the bright colors around us would be to have you with us.*

*I didn't realize it at the time, but the last time I'd worn the bright floral dress I wore to your service was during the summer of 2016, the last time we were at camp together. It has been more than a year. The dress still hangs in my closet, and I haven't worn it since. Maybe it's because my style has changed. Or maybe it still hurts too much.*

*Your family and friends celebrated your life outside, at an orchard in Charlottesville, on a mountain with a splendid view of rolling green hills and tiny red brick houses that looked identical from up high. It was raining when the proceedings first started and the clouds were swirling overhead, heavy and gray, low over the top of the covered terrace where we were gathered to say our goodbyes. They pressed in around us, heavy on our chests, and no matter how much you would have wanted it to be a celebration of life and not a funeral, the air was thick, weighted down by your absence and our tears. All I could think about was how much this wound from Death still ached and how much I wanted you to be here, even though it was the celebration of your life and everyone there knew you were gone, including me.*

*Words made it easier.* As your brothers and your cousin and your dad shared their memories and stories, their words seemed to swirl in the air, to push the clouds back and ease the tightness in my chest. Your cousin told the story of the trampoline she, you, and your brothers used to use, even though it was in someone else's yard and you never asked permission to use it. Someone—I forget who—shared Amy's words about you, and even though I had already read them from her tribute on Facebook, something about hearing them made them real, made them ring true. Hymns from camp swelled in the air, songs I could sing in my sleep and songs I know you loved backed by Valerie's piano music and our voices, the voices of the girls and women who were at camp with you—some that same summer, others from summers past, like me. Words enveloped the covered terrace, loosened the ache in my throat, eased the sting of Death's blow with the balm of reminiscence. I think—I hope—that from wherever you were, wherever you are, you heard our voices, and you sang with us.

By the time we moved to the open stone patio overlooking the rolling hills and tiny houses to raise our glasses in a toast, a chill lingered in the air from the rain, but the sun had peeked through the clouds and was beginning to set, sending long brushstrokes of dusty orange and baby pink across the sky behind gray clouds that were quietly dissolving into soft wisps. Your brother said the timing was fitting, because like you, the sun was a little late—which, despite everything, made everyone laugh—but when it came, it brought true, remarkable beauty, the soft blues and grays of mourning tinged with the warm pinks and oranges of nostalgia and love and hope.

I like to think it was your way of being there, of reminding everyone that even if things could never be the same, they were going to be okay.

\*\*\*

And things are okay, somehow. Weeks have stretched into months, which have stretched into years—a very small number of years, as I write this, but the number doesn't matter so much when you lose someone, because I've never stopped missing you. None of us have. I keep your horseshoe from the summer of 2016 on my desk at school, the program from your service pinned over my bed. There is not a day that goes by where I don't think about you. And, somehow, life keeps moving forward. Losing you still hurts, but the immediacy of it is a little less. I keep those memories, those scraps of images to hold on to. The good things, which make up everything about you.

There's one small thing, though. Even though I went to your service and celebrated your life, I never did get to say goodbye, never got to tell you how much I adored and admired you for being the incredible, spontaneous woman you were for always living life in the moment and to the fullest in the most unexpected ways. I will never get to tell you how badly I want to do my best to live like you—to, in your own handwritten words copied from your journal on the back of the program for your service, live every day like it's my last. And so that wound from Death is still open; it still stings. And I keep holding on, clinging to those fragments of memories because they are all I have left of you and there will be no more for us to make, to help me keep building my portrait of you. I am scared that these fragments will blow away with the wind of age, slip through the cracks in my mind that are sprung from the fallibility of memory even as I know there is no way I could forget about you.

Maybe that's why these stories, your story needed to be written. Because, just maybe, the words to tell this last story *about you were your last gift to me, your way of letting me know that it was okay to write in your honor, to try and capture the colorful whirlwind of your spirit so that I can lock these fragments down. To finally sit down and wrestle with everything I've been feeling since the morning of August 1, 2018, and put it out there in the world. Maybe I haven't found that perfect story because I don't need one, or because it is impossible to capture your whole spirit with just one story. Maybe this is even my way of saying goodbye in the way I never got to in person. We weren't best friends. But you mean a lot to me, and that should be the only validation I need to tell your story.*

*I hope you don't mind that I told it.*

*Missing you always,*
*Karina xxx*

# ACKNOWLEDGMENTS

*This Side of the Veil* would not have been possible without the support, encouragement, and sometimes brutal honesty of so many people. I have to give a special shoutout to the following friends and family:

Alexia, Alise, Alya, Andrew, Liz, and Pascual for being there for and with me since the beginning of everything (and I really mean everything, not just my writing—I mean from primary school to the IB to trying to get us all together during our breaks that somehow only barely overlap);

Catherine, Megan, and Kaylie for our beautiful deep conversations and your endless writerly inspiration;

Annalise, Kat, Justine, and Aliyah for our honest, often confusing late-night conversations that inspired me without you knowing, for always being willing to talk, and for being among my earliest readers;

Alena, Massimo, Natasha, Catie, Morgan, and Olivia for always being there with an encouraging text or Facetime call, especially when we were scattered across the globe and country and each grappling with the fallout of a pandemic;

Ben and Nikki for your early, unfiltered feedback and for your unbridled appreciation that boosted my confidence;

CJ Hauser, Jennifer Brice, and Ndinda Kioko for shaping my writing in beautiful, unexpected ways and for reminding me that I can write anything anywhere at any time, whether it's on the floor in Dulles twenty minutes before my boarding time or on an afternoon train from Berlin to Krakow;

Stephanie and Élodie for being my first supporters in Geneva, for always listening to me and telling me what I need to hear, and for allowing me to believe that I can write my way through the world;

Melody, Heather, and Jennifer for your honest feedback and advice while I was drafting and revising, and for reminding me that I do in fact hold the power over what happens in my own work;

Eric Koester for coaching me and so many other writers through this crazy, unique journey, for giving us authors a space to share the experience, and for encouraging me to take the first step;

Brian and the teams of editors and layout designers at New Degree Press for your support and your answers to my many questions as I fully navigated the world of marketing and publishing for the first time;

Each of you who pre-ordered my collection in April and May (my word limit prevents me from listing all of you, but please know that I deeply appreciate each and every one of you), without whom publication truly would not be possible;

The girls who have come and gone from camp before and after me, who remind me that its ideals do not only live in the valley, but in each of us;

Kanitta, for insights I would never have thought of, for your constant presence through the ups and downs that came before and during the writing and revising this collection, and for your immense talent on the cover concepts;

And Mama and Dada, for listening to me think through feedback out loud and for driving me to always do my best work, believe in myself, and stick to what I know to be true. Thank you, thank you, thank you.

# APPENDIX

*AUTHOR'S NOTE*

TED. "Nora McInerny: We don't 'move on' from grief. We move forward with it." November 2018. Video, 14:43. https://www.ted.com/talks/nora_mcinerny_we_don_t_move_on_from_grief_we_move_forward_with_it?language=en.

Made in the USA
Middletown, DE
07 August 2020